Buffettology:

Profitable investing

Tony Pow

Why you want to read this book

It should improve your financial health substantially.

- This book has over 100 pages (6*9) and is about double the size of its competitors with similar price range.

- This book has been written more than 2 years ago recommending to dump Buffett's funds. If you followed the advice, you would be spared by his current mediocre performance.

- A best seller was written by a young writer whose main income was from his books and none from his investing. Most of my income is from investing.

- Many popular books claiming the authors making millions. However, usually their techniques are hard to follow. Many admitted they had been bankrupted many times. My techniques minimize risking our money. Paper test your technique first.

- There are many popular books combining technical and some fundamentals. They worked very well at one time and folks making millions following the advice. However, look at their recent performances of the last five years.

- One book describes ROE as the only theme (with the story of the life of the author to fill up the book).

My motivation to write this book

I would like to share my experiences, both good and bad. I use simple-to-follow techniques using the free (or low-cost) resources available to us.

Click the link for the articles I wrote for SeekingAlpha.com, a site for investors. http://seekingalpha.com/author/tony-pow/articles

Contents

Why you want to read this book 2

Why you invest 6

Introduction 7

    Disclaimer 12

Section I: Buffett 13

    1   Debunk the myths 13

    2   Preaching that works 19

    3   Search value stocks like Buffett 24

    4   Buffett 25

    5   Efficient charities donation 27

Section II: Simple techniques 29

    How to start 29

    1   Simplest market timing 30

    2   Quick analysis of ETFs 32

    An example 35

    3   Rotate four ETFs 36

    4   Simplest way to evaluate stocks 38

    5   Simplest technical analysis 41

    6   Summary 42

Section III: Find and evaluate stocks 43

    1   Where the web sites are 43

    NASDAQ 44

    Fidelity 45

    2   *Finviz.com screener* 47

    A screener example 48

    Other sources 49

    Common parameters 50

    3   Finviz parameters 55

    Your broker's web site 60

- Quick and dirty 60
  - 5-minute stock evaluation 60
    - Fidelity stock research 62
- 4   Common filters 63
- 5   Sectors to be cautious with 64
- 6   Intangibles 68
- 7   Qualitative analysis 72
- 8   Technical analysis (TA) 76
- 9   Tom's conservative strategy 81
- 10 A turnaround strategy on value stocks 83
- 11 The best strategy 86
  - The second best strategy 88
  - The third strategy 89
  - Buy and monitor 90
- 12 Order prices 92
- 13 When to sell a stock 97

Section IV: Bonus 102
- 1   Market timing example 102
  - Management summary 102
  - Mid-year update 106
  - Canary warning? 108
  - A correction or a crash? 109
- 2   Market timing by calendar 110
- 3   Politics and investing 114

Appendix 1 – All my books 119
Appendix 2 – Complete the Art of Investing 120
- Your choice 123
- Sector Rotation: 21 Strategies 124
- Best stocks to buy for 2021 125

Sell Short Stocks / ETFs 127

China and U.S: Apocalypse or Co-Prosperity 127

Appendix 3 - Our window to the investing world 128

Appendix 4 - ETFs / Mutual Funds 129

Filler: A nightmare?

I got a call from Buffett asking me to lead their stock research.
I asked him why for a nobody; you may be asking the same question. No kidding.

He told me that he should have read my book Scoring Stocks to buy Apple instead of IBM in May, 2013. It would save his company millions of dollars minus $10 for my book. Not to mention the market timing technique that had worked in the last two major market plunges.

I told him, "OK, I'll beat your mediocre returns of the last 5 years."
He said, "You can do better than that and at least beat SPY. If you do so, no one will be that stupid to leave my fund and pay the hefty capital gain taxes."

I told him, "I cannot beat the market as you are the market especially after your expensive fees. In addition, I do not know how to avoid day traders from riding my wagon in trading. Also most of my big profits were made in small stocks that your fund cannot trade besides owning the company."

I woke up trembling. I'm glad it is only a nightmare.

Why you invest

You need to learn about investing sooner or later in your life. You need to take some calculated risks.

Compare the returns of the following assets: cash, CDs, treasury bills, bonds, real estate and stocks. We start with the risk-free investments and end with the riskiest. It turns out that the average returns are in the opposite order. Cash and CDs are not risk-free as inflation eats our profits. For example, the real return is negative for the 2% return in a CD and a 3% inflation rate. In addition you have to pay taxes for the 'returns'. <u>Our capitalist system punishes us for not taking risk</u>.

There are two kinds of risk: blind risk and calculated risk. If you buy a stock due to a recommendation from a commentator on TV or a tip, most likely you are taking a blind risk. It would be the same in buying a house without thoroughly evaluating the house and its neighborhood. When you buy stocks with a proven strategy (i.e. when/what stocks to buy and when/what stocks to sell), you are taking a calculated risk. In the long run, stocks with calculated and educated risks are profitable.

Be a turtle investor by investing in value stocks and holding for longer time periods (a year or more). "Buy and Monitor" is better an approach than "Buy and Hold" as some could lose all the stock values such as in the failure of Enron.

For experienced investors, shorting, short-term trading and covered calls would make you good profits. Simple market timing would reduce your losses during market down turns. If you buy a market ETF and use my simple market timing, you should have beaten the market by a wide margin from 2000 to 2019.

With so many frauds and poor management, do not trust anyone with your investing. Do not buy investing instruments that are highly marketed such as annuity and term insurance.

If you are a handy man and do not mind to satisfy the constant requests of your tenants, buy real estate in growing areas could be very profitable in the long run. Take advantage of the tax laws such as investing in a 401K especially the part that is matched by your company and/or a Roth IRA.

Introduction

This book is about how to profit using Buffett's preaching and how to avoid his strategies that are not applicable to the retail investors and today's market.

I also introduce Swing Trading and how to profit using this strategy. It copies the value investing concept from Buffett and is updated to today's market for retail investors.

Most of my profits in investing are made using the strategy of Swing Trading. Defined by me, Swing Trading is holding the bought stocks for about six months.

Contrary to Buffett's teaching, 'buy-and-hold' is dead since 2000. Before that, we have a nice 10% average return every year. Since then, we have two market crashes with an average loss of about 45%. We need to learn market timing to avoid huge losses. Today, companies have changed too much in a year, so we have to evaluate the market, the sector and the companies more often – I call it 'buy-and-evaluate'.

At the end of the holding period, evaluate the stocks again to determine whether you want to sell it or keep it longer. Last year, most of the stocks are kept for about a year, so they are qualified for the better tax treatment as long-term capital gains in my taxable account.

These stocks should be fundamentally sound (i.e. value stocks). Hence they need at least six months for the market to realize their values. Select the holding period that fits your objective.

After six months, the fundamentals of the company, the sector that the company belongs to and/or the market may change. Hence, we need to evaluate and decide the 'buy/hold' decision. Sometimes, you may want to raise cash to buy another stock that has more appreciation potential than a stock you own. Churning the portfolio improves the quality of your portfolio.

When the market is going to plunge, do not buy stocks. I have a simple chart to identify market plunges (See my book on Market Timing). It depends on stock data, so it will not identify the peaks and the bottoms precisely, but it will spare you for further losses and will instruct you when to reenter the market. It worked for the last two market crashes. It will detect the next crash, and hopefully it will give us enough time to react as the last two.

After we have decided that the market is not risky, screen stocks for further evaluation. I use fundamental metrics to screen stocks. Then look for intangibles and do a thorough qualitative analysis on each screened stock. There is no magic formula, but due diligence will pay off in the long run. This book does not promise overnight wealth as promised by many others.

This book is intended for a retail investor and I am one myself. It is not written by a journalist who may never make a buck in the market.

I have conducted exhaustive simulations to back-test these strategies over the past 12 years. I am not a writer but a retail investor similar to most of my readers. I've been making a comfortable living via my investment ideas that I'm sharing in this book.

The strategies described here have been used in my book Best Stocks 2014, According to Me. From 12/16/13 (the publish date) to 3/4/14, the list of all 135 selected stocks beat SPY by 103% and the list of 9 small cap stocks beat SPY by 500%.

My additions to conventional swing trading

Hopefully my additions improve the performance of a strategy that already works.

- I add market timing to Swing Trading. You need to sell most stocks during a market plunge (of course better selling at the peak) and buy them back when the chart indicates so (see my book on Market Timing).
- Diversify your portfolio. Keep less than 15 stocks for a portfolio less than a million. Ensure not more than 3 stocks in the same sector. Keep 20 stocks for portfolio over a million. Too many stocks would require more of your time that would be better spent in evaluating stocks. Too few stocks would impact your portfolio when one stock has a big loss.
- Stick with stocks over $2, average daily volume over 8,000 shares (or 6,000 shares for price over $20) and market cap over 200

million in the major three exchanges for my swing strategy based on fundamentals.

Most big winners usually are in the price range between $2 and $12 price, and market cap between 200 million to 800 million. These stocks are ignored by the institution investors due to their restrictions. There are exceptions. Adjust the criteria according to your requirements.

- Ignore the subscription services claiming making more than 30% profit consistently. Some even have examples of making 5,000%. Most likely they tell you the winners but not their losers. When they back test their strategies, they cheat their performances with survivorship bias (i.e. those bankrupt stocks are not in the historical database). If their returns are that great, do you think they will share their secrets with you?
- Some made a big fortune and lost it all. So, the turtles that make small profits consistently and keep all the wins fare far better.

For beginner investors

Read basic investment articles for beginners. Both Fidelity and AAII (both require being a client or a member) have excellent articles. Alternatively, buy a book for beginners. To include all the basic terms and concepts, I have to double the size of this book which is already lengthy and bore most readers who already have the basic knowledge.

Click here for Morningstar classroom.
http://morningstar.com/cover/classroom.html

Click here for Fidelity basic in investing.
https://www.fidelity.com/investment-guidance/investing-basics

How this book is organized

Most graphs and tables are in landscape orientation (recommended for small screens) for both paperback and e-readers. Some graphs may not be displayed adequately on a small screen of an e-reader. E-readers may be available in the current version of Windows, so you can read e-books on the larger screen of your PC. For better orientation, just flip the e-readers 90 degrees. Some reader lets you select a table or a graph to display it to fit the screen.

A link is usually included for the most screens. Copy it to your browser to display the graphs on your PC if desirable. Instructions on how to produce some graphs are provided as you should try them out. One example is how to produce a chart on detecting market crashes.

The **font size** (Ctrl Minus for browser implementation of e-readers) and line spacing of most e-book formats can be adjusted. The unknown, special character is the "smiling face" that the current Kindle does not convert correctly as of this writing.

There are clickable links to web articles. Most of them are from my own web sites and public web sites such as Wikipedia. Some public links may not be available in the future as they are not under my control and my book offerings may change.

These links extend the usefulness of this book by making available specific topics that may not be interesting to every reader. It also provides articles (most are not written by me) for more in-depth analyzes.

Fidelity Video provides video clips to explain some basic terms and it may require Fidelity customers to sign on in order to view them. Check the trial offer from Fidelity. YouTube offers similar video lessons.

The current version provides most of the links the paperback readers can enter into your browser. Get the same information by entering a search in Wikipedia such as Dogs of Dow.

Investopedia is another source beside Wikipedia.
http://www.investopedia.com/

'Afterthoughts' includes my additional comments and ideas of minor importance.

There are fillers with tips, refreshing pictures (taken by me) and jokes (most original) to fill up the empty space of the printed book. Fillers, links and afterthoughts may disrupt the flow of reading this book. However, no readers so far ask me to take them out even in the digitized version of this book. Many page breaks have been eliminated to improve the flow of the book.

For convenience, this book uses SPY, an Exchange Traded Fund (ETF) simulating the S&P 500 index, as the benchmark for the market.

Annualized returns (Return * 365 / (Days between)) are used where appropriate for more meaningful comparison. To illustrate, I have a 10% return in 6 months, a 10% in a year and a 10% in 2 years. It is more meaningful to use annualized returns of 20%, 10% and 5% respectively in this example.

Usually I do not include the dividend, so you can add an estimated 1.5% to the annualized return. In addition, compound interest is not used for easier calculation, so the actual return could be even better. Many of my tests are not detailed in this book but their summaries are. It reduces the size of this book that is already huge.

About the author

I graduated from Cal. State University at San Jose in Industrial Engineering and University of Mass. in Amherst with a MS in Industrial Engineering. My last job was in IT. I have been an investor for over 30 years.

Dedication
To all retail investors and future retail investors including my grandchildren.

Acknowledgement

Thanks to Seeking Alpha, Fidelity, Wikipedia and Investopedia for the many helpful links to enrich this book.

Yahoo!Finance and Finviz.com for the tools and charts used in this book. Poi for gathering my research info and working on the business side of the book.

Important notices
© 2014-2021 Tony Pow. Emails to pow_tony@yahoo.com.

Version	Paperback	eBooks
1.0	08/14	08/14
2.0	08/16	08/16
3.0	06/19	06/19
3.2	01/21	01/21

No part of this book can be reproduced in any form without the written approval of the author.

Book store managers can order this book from Createspace.com.
https://tonyp4idea.blogspot.com/2020/12/book-managers.html

Book update.
https://ebmyth.blogspot.com/2020/12/updates-for-all-books.html

If this book is thinly sized, imagine how the Kindle version of "Complete the art of investing" with about 850 pages (6*9) would help you financially. That could be the best $10 you invest in.

Disclaimer

Do not gamble with money that you cannot afford to lose. Past performance is a guideline and is not necessarily indicative of future results. All information is believed to be accurate, but there it is not a guarantee. All the strategies including charts to detect market plunges described have no guarantee that they will make money and they may lose money. Do not trade without doing due diligence and be warned that most data may be obsolete. All my articles and the associated data are for informational and illustration purposes only. I'm not a professional investment counselor or a tax professional. Seek one before you make any investment decisions. The above mentioned also applies for all other advice such as on accounting, taxes, health and any topic mentioned in this book. I am not a professional in any of these fields. Most of the time, I use annualized for a better comparison; 5% in a month is more than 4% in a year for example. For simplicity, most of my returns do not include commissions, exchange fees, order spread and dividends. Same for all the links contained in this book. Some articles may offend some one or some organization unintentionally. If I did, I'm sorry about that. I am politically and religiously neutral. I provide my best efforts to ensure the accuracy of my articles. Data also from different sources was believed to be accurate. However, there is no guarantee that they are accurate and suitable for the current market conditions and /or your individual situations. My publisher and I are not liable for any damages in using this book or its contents.

Section I: Buffett

This book has been written more than 2 years ago recommending to dump Buffett's funds. If you followed the advice, you would be spared by his current mediocre performance. In 2015, Buffett performed very poorly. Buffett usually does not invest on companies whose products he does not understand. He did not use smart phones and emails. Hence, he has not invested in market-beating high-tech companies such as Apple, Microsoft, Netflix, Facebook and Google.

1 Debunk the myths

Buffett Mania

Traditionally, growth stocks have higher P/Es than value stocks, but the reverse is sometimes true. As of 11/25/13, the expected P/Es (from Finviz.com) of some randomly-picked stocks were:

Growth Stocks	Expected P/E	Value Stocks	Expected P/E
Cisco	10	Coca-Cola (KO)	18
Apple	11	Colgate-Palmolive (CL)	21
San Disk	12	Verizon (VZ)	14
Average	**11**		**18**

I suspect it is caused by Buffett and his followers coupled with dividend stock seekers. During this period, dividend stocks had beaten the low interest rates from bonds and CDs. KO, CL, VZ and many others belong to the stocks that Buffett would own. They all gave dividends and had an edge such as brand name recognition and monopoly that Buffett loved. The above are only small samples of these stocks in the respective category. To me, Buffett Mania (my term) is a mild bubble and I expect the average Expected P/E of growth stocks would be over 15 in 2016 (today in 2020, they should be around 25).

This mania will not continue as we're running out of these stocks to buy. I do not believe there will be opportunity to buy them at 50% discount (as Buffett preaches) unless we've a market crash. When a strategy is over-used, they will not be effective. No exception.

The Reality

Warren Buffett is one of the premier investors in our generation if not the best. However, I believe that some of his practices are not applicable to today's market and to us, the retail investors.

Most of the money earned was for himself and not for the stock holders of Berkshire in the last three years. SPY, an ETF simulating the S&P 500 index, offers greater diversity and has seen less volatility as of this writing. If Buffett is such a hero in picking stocks, then those who constantly beat the S&P 500 Index by a sizable margin are better investor heroes, and there are many. We need to constantly scrutinize whom we listen to.

Performance Comparison

As of 11/1/2013, the average annualized return for the last 3 years:

BRKA	SPY
10%	11%

SPY (the market to most) gives an annual dividend of about 1.5% (about 1.9% this year) and BRKA does not. Not even beating SPY from a primer investor is just mediocre.

Why Buffett's current mediocre performance is important

I do not care how much money he made 10 years ago but what he will make in the next 10 years. Many have been utterly convinced by the many books written on his achievements many years ago. The most important to us: Are his strategies still relevant to us today?

When Peter Lynch (managing the Magellan Fund, 5/1977 to 5/1990) lost his golden touch and he quit the job, I got my money out! Most investors did not even after experiencing several years of poor returns (compared to his previous incredible performances). The result was many years of mediocre returns for the fund. Hence, Buffett's mediocre performance in the last three years matters and it could be the canary to his future performance.

Many of his teachings are still relevant and they are described in the next article. The following of his practices are to be debunked. I just want to seek the truth. Am I dumb to argue with the most famous investor? Read the following with an open mind and decide it yourself.

Debunk the Myths

- 'Never sell.'

    The "Buy and Hold" strategy has been dead since 2000 to me. The fundamentals of most companies change after a decade or so and some even earlier.

    Market timers can detect and take advantage of the market crashes using market timing. Most books and comments that praise this strategy are based on data before 2000. This strategy should be at least replaced by "Buy and Monitor".

    Buffett made big money in KO in the first 10 years of his ownership, but not a lot in the next 10 years. If he cashed in after 10 years of ownership and then bought another stock with similar performance, he would have made far, far more.

    I prefer to churn my portfolio to reflect the current market conditions. Buffett's ownership in The Washington Post (sold in recent year) was amazing then, but it could be too risky now. The paper is facing the losing battle against the free internet.

    Market fundamentals perpetually change! To illustrate this, there were ten well-known department stores ten years ago, and now only Macy's survives; most others were acquired or bankrupted. The acquired ones may fare better. However, you need to analyze them again whether the combined company still fits your requirements and objectives. The internet enables Amazon.com to capture the retail sector. Most profitable companies in the last ten years such as Apple and Facebook are related to the internet and not your daddy's traditional companies.

    There are so many examples to debunk the evergreen concept such as AIG, BlockBuster, HPQ and GE. The market is changing with new technology and competition. We cannot buy and sit back enjoying the present appreciation and dividends.

I read an outdated but popular book by a very famous author. A very good portion of his recommended stocks have not survived. Most his stocks had great appreciation in the year after his recommendation, but not after a few years. It is another argument for "Buy and Monitor".

If you do not sell, you do not have cash to buy stocks when the market is cheap.

It is better to understand the new products and their profit potentials, and then make your decisions accordingly. Buffett should depend more on his extensive resources and his many analysts who should have diverse disciplines. Most highly-profitable stocks will not be matured companies but small companies with innovative products.

- 'Rule #1. Do not lose money. Rule #2. Do not forget rule #1.'

If every stock bought is risk-free, the return could not be good; it fits into "nothing risked, nothing gained". It is similar to buying Treasury Bills that have no loss in theory. However, holding Treasury Bills until maturity loses buying power due to inflation. Our capitalist system punishes us for not taking risk, same is trading stocks.

Evaluate the ratio of "return / risk" to see whether the expected return is justified for the risk. If the chance to lose 50% is the same as gaining more than 100%, then the risk is justified. It is not a science, but probability theory and common sense are decent tools. In the long term it usually works. In addition, one's personal risk tolerance determines his/her investment methods. Most retirees should be conservative.

- 'Margin of safety'.

The margin of safety is equal to the difference between the stock price and the intrinsic value, which is quite easy to obtain from many web sites. From my limited test, this metric does not beat the market most of the time.

There will be too few stocks to buy if everyone treats margin of safety as the first priority. It worked for Buffett before as few followed his 'margin of safety' practice.

Many institutional investors follow Buffett's preaching as they learn it in colleges; they drive the market. When you follow the herd, you will not beat the market.

During a secular bull market, the market would favor momentum and growth over value and hence 'margin of safety' will not be appropriate. However, it would work better in a secular bear market.

- 'Think of Stocks as a Business'.

I do not have the time to run so many companies I owned. I do not fire employees, do not have legal obligations, do not make day-to-day decisions, etc. I can sell the stock with a click of the button with no emotion and no legal liabilities attached. Do you really think your ideas and/or votes on how to run the company will influence the management's decisions? It may work for Buffett as he owns part and sometimes the whole company.

Running a business is very different from investing in a company. Do not be confused! Investors' only objective is to make a profit with the least risk. The officers of a company are liable to frauds and negligence but not the stock holders.

When a company bankrupts, most sole owners bankrupt too financially and mentally. The stock holder does not suffer the same at least not in the same degree. You may have many other assets, stocks and/or a job. You do not have to tell your loyal employees to leave. No lenders will call you unless you buy the stock on margins.

With an optimal portfolio of 20 stocks, it is not possible to run 20 companies simultaneously. I have never attended the earnings announcement and never talked to CEOs and/or their investor relationship representative. How much it would cost for the air fares and the hotels 4 times a year for 20 companies?

- Buffett's portfolio.

It is not <u>diversified</u> enough (especially in his early years). However, the portfolio under his insurance company might be.

When he trades, he pays extra due to his huge volumes. He usually buys the entire company and most retail investors never do that.

- Main brands represent matured companies that will give good dividends but usually have limited growth. When they do not perform, the stock will plunge. IBM is a recent example that Buffett owns. The 'cloud' technology is risky and not highly profitable at least for now for IBM.

  The most profitable and riskiest companies are penny stocks. Buffett could reap the profits with their analytical skills. He chooses to stay away from most of them as they are too small for his portfolio.

- He may miss many of current strategies that work such as market timing, momentum strategy, technical analysis, insider trading, high tech companies, turnarounds and investing in small companies, etc. They are all described in this book.

  During the peak or during the plunge, we should accumulate cash that is needed to purchase stocks when the bottom is obvious. Market timing is our tool. If it works more than 50% of the time, we should make good profits. My market timing works two times from 2000 to 2010 with one false signal that told us to exit but return shortly.

- Buffett avoids growth companies. He does not have Microsoft, Apple and Google in his portfolio. Google represents one of the most appreciated stocks in the last 10 years. Google is expensive by the fundamental metrics. However, it is a growth stock with technology that Buffett may not appreciate. FAANG (Facebook, Apple, Amazon, Netflix and Google) are doing well recently and they are included in major indexes. That's one reason why Buffett cannot beat the indexes most of the time.
- Some argue that Buffett's performance is better during market plunges. It is true for most value stocks. However, you can perform better by staying in cash or even investing in contra ETFs when the market timing tell you so.
- Buffett's huge portfolio from his insurance company is the market and you cannot beat yourself after the hefty fees.

- As of 2016, dividend stocks that are favored by Buffett could be a mild bubble. When the interest rates are hiked, the dividend stocks would return to its historical values.
- There are too many followers on Buffett and it could create a bubble; all bubbles will be burst sooner or later.
- Graham's (Buffett's teacher) preaching worked decades ago, but it may not work today as the market conditions are quite different.
- Many high tech products and drugs are hard to understand. We should not ignore them because we do not understand their products.

Afterthoughts

- The stock holders of his funds may have to pay a lot of capital gain taxes when they sell them.
- When the day Buffett dies, will his funds plunge?

2   Preaching that works

Many of Buffett's preaching still works fine today. However, some need to be discussed further so we can use them effectively.

- Identify exceptional companies with durable competitive advantage.

  These are the companies with high profit margins such as Coke. Even Coke has Pepsi as its major competitor. These companies usually are matured companies and give generous dividends. They do not have to plow back all their cash into research and development. Very few (Microsoft is one) high-tech companies and drug companies belong to the group. Most use the profits to build the next better mouse traps instead of giving out dividends. Should we ignore these companies? I do not ignore them, but Buffett would.

  Washington Post is one of these matured companies. However, the internet is changing all its advantage as most of us get our news analyses free from the internet. In addition, cutting down trees to make paper is not good for the environment. [Update: Buffett sold Washington Post.]

  We need to monitor the companies that we have stocks on such as GE, Lehman Brothers, Enron and Boeing. When bad news are really bad, sell the stocks right away as they could go to zero.

Microsoft is in this category monopolizing PC operating system and Office, the most-used business software. I wonder why it is not in Buffett's portfolio and may be Gates could give him a good friendly pointer during their bridge games. Buffett still has not bought Apple and Google as of this writing. He has missed these profit opportunities. According to Buffett, Microsoft, Apple and Google are not the companies with 'durable competitive advantage'. I have to disagree.

There are many innovative companies that will not fit into Buffett's 'exceptional criteria'. When they plow back most earnings to research / development, these companies usually do not have good net profits and they do not give generous dividends.

To illustrate this, BSX is one of them finding cures to chronic pains. I read an article on the company from my Sunday paper. Even I did not (and even today) really know how it worked, but I was excited enough to buy its stock two times without doing any research (not recommended) in Oct., 2012. As of today (8/2013), it is up by more than 100%.

I will buy these 'exceptional' companies if I can find them. I will sell them when their price appreciation potentials have peaked or there are better stocks to buy.

- Get most info from financial statements.

Today many web sites such as Finviz.com and your broker's include most of the financial data and ratios. Buffett loses his edge as all these data are available to everyone. We do not have to read through the financial statements for these data. However, we do have to be careful:

1. Ensure the ratios derived from these financial statements are up-to-date. Usually the company's web site provides the most updated data.

2. Comparative ratios in the same sector. Many web sites provide this information. To illustrate this, Price / Sale has different meaning between a super market and a drug company. The former makes money by selling at low profit margins.

3. It is still important to read the footnotes and 'extraordinary' items such as those one-time charges. Settling a major lawsuit could be a one-time charge. When a virtual asset is out of ordinary, be careful.

Success in investing today is not solely on how to get the information and understand the financial ratios. We should separate the good data from garbage, and evaluate all the immense data that are readily available from the internet. I recommend to pay attention to insiders' purchases.

- Never sell.

I have presented my opposing views on "Never Sell" philosophy in my last chapter. However, sometimes it has its merits. There are many companies that Buffett had or has incredible returns after holding for over 10 years such as Washington Post (sold recently), American Express and Coke to name a few. Personally I usually sold my big winners too early. I should use stops to protect my profits during their uptrends.

Very seldom I have stocks making over 300% as I usually sell them after they make over 100%; TTWO is an exception which is gifted to my grandchildren. I keep my gainers for at least a year in taxable accounts to take advantage of the more favorable taxes on long-term capital gains. Buffett is a living example that his strategy works at least 5 years ago. We need to identify why this strategy works and whether it is still applicable to retail investors and the current market conditions. Several thoughts:

1. These companies usually have been analyzed fully for its long-term appreciation potential. Do you have the time and the knowledge to do so? If not, depend on some reputable subscriptions and/or buy ETFs.

2. He has great vision to see the real potential of a company. Do you have that vision? However, he has missed many profitable stocks recently.

3. Institutional investors have thorough research than us. However, most institutional investors can only trade on large companies. That is why we should consider small stocks but not penny stocks.

Today commission costs are very low (even free from Fidelity and Charles Schwab) and we can postpone taxes on capital gains from non-taxable accounts (none from Roth IRAs).

- Buy the stocks at 50% discount

Stocks are manipulated to cause temporary price erosions.

This strategy makes him and his teacher Graham a lot of money. As opposed to Graham, Buffett still holds these stocks longer even if they have not appreciated in one or two years. He seldom sells these stocks and many times his patience pays off.

My suggestion is some stocks will stay low forever for good reasons. I recommend to repeat the same evaluation on your purchased stocks every 6 months. Hold them if the fundamentals are not deteriorating. The stock prices of some bad companies could go to zero. Use stops to protect your stock holdings. Buffett's stocks are usually value stocks and very seldom they go to zero. However, we have several big companies' stocks go to zero recently.

It is similar to buying quality companies when everyone is selling in fear. The best profit opportunity is buying quality stocks at the market bottom (easily said than done). Determining the market bottom is impossible, but there are some hints that may help us to determine whether the market is plunging.

When a company has 2 billion dollar cash and its market cap is 1 billion, most likely it is mispriced. There are exceptions such as a pending serious lawsuit.

- Buy a good business with a good management at a discount.

There are many companies on sale in 2000 and 2007. Need to separate gems from companies that would go bankrupt such as many internet companies in 2000. If the problem that causes the company to lose more than half of the value is temporary, then it could be a good buy betting on turnaround.

A good management is required for Buffett as he seldom wants to manage the company. Many companies go bankrupted because of frauds and / or poor management. It is a good sign that the owners have a good stake in their own companies. It is a bad sign when the CEO is over-paid compared to his peers and / or lives lavishly with huge loans from his company.

- Learn from mistakes.
  He made several mistakes as every investor did. He sold the businesses in re-insurance, airline, etc. but he seldom made the same mistake again. Learn from how he deals with his mistakes.

- He does not follow hot fad such as the internet in 2000. I prefer to follow it (a.k.a. momentum investing), but have an exit plan and protect profits via stops.

- Evaluate stocks with common sense. Mathematical models on stock evaluations are for professors to have a job and they never resemble real life.

- Buffett has switched between bonds and stocks successfully. Most of the time, he was not the first one to exit, but he adapted to the market conditions better than most of us. He usually pays more, but it had turned out many times he was right.

- Buffett as a person has a lot for us to learn from. He is frugal and generous. Making money is his career and hobby, not because he loves to make money for worldly stuffs.

- Buffett has his share of bad investing decisions such as buying IBM instead of buying Google, Microsoft and Apple.

- According to Buffett and Peter Lynch, they had been misled more often than getting meaningful information by calling/visiting CEOs. In addition, most of us cannot even reach anyone important in large companies.

3   Search value stocks like Buffett

Buffett stresses on value and would like to buy these companies at 25% off their intrinsic values, which are quite hard to determine. There are many screens simulated on how Buffett finds stocks. You should paper trade the stocks screened from these screens and check the performances after at least 6 months. Here are some common parameters in these screens. I also recommend do not buy any stocks during market plunges.

- ROE. Check out the ROEs for the last 5 to 10 years, not just the most recent year.
- D/E. Low Debt/Equity.
- Profit Margin.
- Competitive advantage. The less competition, the better.
- Longevity. At least in business for 10 years.

From the above, Buffett cannot find too many stocks to buy during a bull market. He also ignores a lot of startups and high tech companies. His portfolio should produce stable but not amazing performance.

In addition, he needs good managers who should be kind to his employees, paying back to the society and not using his company as his ATM besides business smart.

Using the Patriots franchise for illustration purposes, the Sullivan family did not make money even on Michael Jackson's concert in New England while everyone made good money. After Kraft took over (paying too high a price to many), the franchise turned around and became the most successful and profitable one under his helm.

Afterthoughts

There are so many books on Buffett. Glance through them in the book stores and pick up those strategies that fit your investing philosophy and style. Many of his techniques are not applicable to retail investors, so be selective. His yearly announcement reports show his insights, discipline and knowledge.

As of 2020, these books are not too popular as they used to be.

4   Buffett

With utmost respect, Buffett's ideas may not be valid to us, the average retail investors, for the following reasons.

- We do not make big bets such as buying most or all of a company.
- He cannot usually buy small-cap stocks, which are proven to be better performers in the long run.
- He has connections and sweetheart deals that most of us do not have access to.
- We can dump losers or winners any time we want without public opinions on our trades.
- Most of his bets require him to pay extra to get in and get out.

There are exceptions. You should make money by following him to buy Petro China and several other companies. However, he has his share of losers. As of 15/2016, he had not beaten the major index for the last five years, quite a long time for investors.

Contrary to Mr. Buffett's philosophy, I believe buy-and-hold is dead after 2000 for experienced investors. Most books / articles defending buy-and-hold are based on data before 2000. The market changes so fast that a good company could become unprofitable due to circumstances beyond its control or just due to bad management. With market timing, we can avoid some of the hefty losses in 2000 and 2007.

Insurance sector is a black swan to me. When something unexpected happens once in a blue moon, it would spoil all the fun and profit. Reinsurance companies (insuring insurers) are even riskier.

If Buffett only handled a portfolio of $10 million or so, he would beat most of us year after year by a good margin. No one including Peter Lynch can make a decent return with this huge portfolio. Lynch quit and Buffett continues, so I give Buffett more credit.

We can learn a lot from many of Buffett's sound investing philosophy / ideas and he has proven to be the greatest investor in our time. His yearly reports should benefit all investors. Many have made over 10,000% investing with Buffett but none in the last five years. He gains my respect by managing such a large portfolio. You cannot beat yourself when you are the market. I also respect him for donating most his money to charities.

These days Buffett seems acting like a running dog for Obama, or he is blinded by all the glorious articles written about him, his money and his good deeds. He should concentrate on running his company whose performance has not beaten the market lately as he used to. Alternately he should retire to concentrate on his preaching about taxes and the government issues even some are controversial.

He did a great job in raising his children to be independent. However, I do not agree with his advice to the girl to be a business woman instead of a doctor who could cure thousands and save many lives.

High taxes have been proven bad for the economy and the stock market throughout our history. As opposed to the middle class, the rich have many tricks from their tax lawyers to avoid taxes. They can pass their wealth to their children and charities that allow their children to draw incomes from.

Somehow it reminds me of the Peter's Principle: When you're promoted to some job position you're not capable of, you do not perform as before.

Afterthoughts

- The announcement of the retirement of the CEO of Microsoft boosted the stock by about 7% in a day. I cannot believe it means about 20 billion dollars added to the market cap of Microsoft. What will happen to the stocks of Buffett's company when he retires or dies?

- Funny article on Buffett.
  http://buzzonomics.wordpress.com/2013/08/30/jokes-facts-and-words-of-wisdom-from-warren-buffett/

5 Efficient charities donation

We do not give money to an addict, because we figure that they will use it to further their addition. It is the same when we leave money to our government in various forms of taxes. They will spend it recklessly.

We should teach the poor how to fish instead of giving them fish for their entire lives. We should use a model specific to Africa (such as the one from China) instead of the American model to Africa. Helping the poor is not a science but an art. Throwing money at the problem will not solve it long-term.
.
As Howard Buffett, Warren Buffett's son said, once Americans leave with the big machines / equipment, Africans will return to the bad old days. You do not need to automate aggressively when abundance of cheap labor is available. From his ideas on Africa I watched on TV, I think he has better insight and vision to handle his father's foundation than anyone else.

I believe that he would contribute more to the world by heading the charity instead of running his father's company. He seems to have little interest and desire to run his father's company from his conversation in the TV news magazine "60 Minutes". Making another billion is not a big deal but helping another African to survive is to him. Warren Buffett's greatest contribution to the society as well as the world is having raised great children like Howard with proper values that our society is lacking.

The donations from Warren Buffet and Bill Gates are the noblest deed to mankind. I argue against the comments that they profit themselves. Of course, both should donate their appreciated stocks so they can maximize their donations. They should appoint their heirs to supervise their foundations and get salaries for the work to ensure the foundation is administered properly. Do you want a high school dropout or a welfare recipient to handle your foundation?

The African farming industry is being destroyed as they cannot compete with the overwhelming impact of donations. How can the African farmers compete with freebies? Often donations are skimmed by the corrupt officials like many in Haiti and some African countries.

Try to identify the charities with low overheads and utilizing the contributions most efficiently. Some charities spend over one third of the contributions on its employees' pensions and salaries; some even use 99% of the contribution for themselves. With limited funds, try to limit yourself to one charity. The main cause of their high overhead is their various marketing campaigns to solicit donations, such as via (junk) mail, telephone solicitations, etc. Also be aware of their executive compensation scheme.

The United States and its citizens are the most generous and hope it remains so. Donate cash rather than merchandise. Donating winter clothes to Africa is very silly. Donating human milk could be damaging the health of the babies. The bottle water donated costs more to ship. Use common sense - not just make you feel better!

As Gandhi said, the world has enough resources for all but we're not unselfish enough to share.

Afterthoughts
Fidelity has a charity account that is quite easy to open. Remember donating appreciated securities would make the biggest bang for the buck. Check the current tax laws.

Most Americans are generous and educated. I was touched when some perfect strangers helping the elderly. I was helped (even I was not that old) when I had a flat tire.

The poor are admitted to nursing homes free of charge. The middle class like me may not afford to go to nursing homes. It defers my donation to charities as I have to ensure I have enough savings to go to a nursing home if I need to go.

Links
China.
http://www.tonyp4idea.blogspot.com/2009/11/china-helps-african-countries.html

Howard.
http://www.cbsnews.com/8301-18560_162-57456243/howard-buffett-farming-and-finance/

Haiti.
http://en.wikipedia.org/wiki/Haiti#Economy

Section II: Simple techniques

For starters, just trade ETFs such as SPY (an ETF simulating the market), and you can skip the rest of the book. It only take a few minutes every month. When the market is not plunging, buy or keep SPY (or any ETF that stimulates the market); otherwise sell it. Do the opposite when the market is recovering.

If you have less than $50,000 to invest, just buy ETFs. Improve your investing skills by reading investment articles from this book and your broker's web site. For example, Fidelity has a lot of information for investors.

Subscription to AAII is recommended. When your portfolio grows more than $50,000, invest on a subscription such as Value Line, GuruFocus, Zacks or IBD (more for momentum traders). Initially, use the information for paper trading on value stocks, which is usually available from brokers.

For the long term, knowledge is most important in your investing life and experience comes next. Retail investors have a lot of advantages over fund managers. However, I advise you NOT to be a trader. Hence, you should ignore the 'fabulous' trade systems that claim to be very profitable. Statistically most amateur traders lose money as they cannot compete with experienced, disciplined traders.

How to start

I recommend trading ETFs first and when the market is not risky. The very basic terms such as ETF are not fully explained here; try Investopedia for terms you need to know. Otherwise this book would be doubled in size and it would bore most readers. Investopedia, your broker's web site (especially Fidelity) and AAII (requiring subscription) provide many excellent articles. Alternatively, buy a book for beginners. Here are some freebies:

Click here for Morningstar classroom.
http://morningstar.com/cover/classroom.html
Click here for Vanguard.
https://investor.vanguard.com/investing/investor-education
Click here for Investopedia's Tutorials.
http://www.investopedia.com/university/
Click here for Yahoo!
http://finance.yahoo.com/education/begin_investing
Click here for Fidelity basic in investing.
https://www.fidelity.com/investment-guidance/investing-basics

1 Simplest market timing

Why market timing

Before 2000, market timing was a waste of time. However after that, we have had two market plunges with the average loss of about 45%. It sounds harder to time the market than it actually is. We have a simple technique to detect market plunges and when to reenter the market. Our objective is reducing the loss to 25%.

Market timing depends on charts; the following describes how to use chart information without creating charts. Most charts will not identify the peaks and bottoms of the market as they depend on data (i.e. the stock prices). However, it would reduce further loses. It is simpler than it sounds. Just follow the procedure below.

The first part of this technique detects market plunges, and the second part advises you when to reenter the market. It applies to individual stocks too. It also works to detect the trend of a sector (entering an ETF for the specific sector instead of SPY) and a specific stock.

How to detect market plunges without charts (a.k.a. <u>Death Cross</u>)
1. Bring up Finviz.com.

2. Enter SPY (or any ETF that simulates the market) or RSP for equally weighed SPY.

3. If SMA-200% is positive, it indicates that the market plunge has not been detected and you can skip the following steps.

4. The market is plunging if SMA-50% is more negative than SMA-200%. To illustrate this condition, SMA-200% is -2% and SMA-50% is -5%.

5. Sell most stocks starting with the riskiest ones first such as the ones with negative earnings, high P/Es and/or high Debt/Equity. Obtain this info from Finviz.com by entering the symbol of the stock you own.

6. Conservative investors should sell only those over-priced stocks. Aggressive investors should sell all stocks. Extremely aggressive investors should sell all stocks, buy contra ETFs, and even short stocks. I do not recommend beginners to be aggressive.

When to return to the market (a.k.a. Golden Cross)

Use the above in a reversed sense to detect whether the market has been recovering. However, when the SMA-200% turns positive, I would start buying value stocks (low P/E but the 'E' has to be positive, and/or low Debt/Equity).

1. Bring up Finviz.com.
2. Enter SPY (or any ETF that simulates the market).
3. If SMA-200% is negative, the market is not recovering, and you can skip the following steps.
4. Sell all contra ETFs and close all shorts if you have any.
5. Market recovery is confirmed when SMA-50% is more positive than SMA-200%. To illustrate this condition, SMA-200% is 2% and SMA-50% is 5%. Commit a large percent of cash (or all cash for aggressive investors) to stocks. If you do not know what to buy, buy SPY or an ETF that simulates the market.

How often to check the market timing indicators

Do the above once a month. When the SPY price is closer to SMA actions percentage, perform the above once a week. The charts and data for market timing described in this book are based on SMA-350 (Simple Moving Average) that is more preferable than this simple procedure, but it requires some simple charting.

Nothing is perfect
If the market timing is perfect, there would be no poor folks. The major 'defects' are:

- It does not detect the peak / bottom as it depends on past data. However, it would save you a lot during the crash.
- It is hard to determine whether it is a correction or a crash.
- From 2000 to 2010, there is only one false signal. The indicator tells you to exit and then tell you reenter the market shortly. In most cases, you do not lose a lot. After 2010, we have more false signals.
- The market may not be rational or may be influenced due to specific conditions such as excessive printing of USD.

2 Quick analysis of ETFs

Evaluate an ETF

ETFs are a basket of stocks according to the market, a specific sector, country or a specific theme.

Yahoo!Finance used to give the P/E of an ETF. Try to get it from ETFdb.com. Enter the symbol of the ETF such as XLU, and then select Valuation. If it is below 15 and above zero, it could be a value ETF. Also, if the current price is lower than its NAV, it is sold at a discount (or premium vice versa). Compare its YTD Return to SPY's.

Alternatively, get similar info from http://www.multpl.com/. In addition, this web site provides the following metrics: Shiller P/E, Price/Sales, and Price/Book.

From Finviz.com, enter the ETF symbol. If SMA-20%, SMA-50% and SMA-200% are all positive, most likely the ETF is in an uptrend. To illustrate, SMA-200 is Simple Moving Average for the last 200 trading sessions (no trading on weekends and specific holidays). The percent is how much the stock price of the ETF is above the SMA. If the percent is negative, it means the stock price is below the SMA.

If your average holding period of your stocks is about 50 days, SMA-50% is more appropriate to you.

If RSI(14) > 65, it is probably over-sold; if it is < 30, it is probably under-sold (indicating value).

In addition, ensure the ETF's average volume is high (I suggest more than 10,000 shares), the market cap is more than 300 M, and it has low fees. Most popular ETFs have these characteristics. Beginners should avoid leveraged ETFs.

How to determine if the sector has been recovered

It is easier to profit by following the uptrend of an ETF using the above info. It is hard to detect when the bottom of an ETF has been reached. If SMA-20%, SMA-50% and SMA-200% are all positive, most likely the ETF is in an uptrend or it has recovered. It does not always happen as predicted, so use stops to protect your investment.

An example

First, determine whether the market is risky. Most beginners should not invest in a risky market. Advanced investors can bet against the market or a specific sector by buying contra ETFs or puts.

Next, you want to limit the number of sector ETFs by selecting those that are either in an uptrend or hitting bottom (bottom is hard to predict). Personally I prefer sectors with long-term uptrends (indicated by articles found in many web sites including cnnfn.com and Seeking Alpha.

For illustration purposes only for deteriorating market conditions, I would select the following ETFs: SPY (simulating the market based on large companies) and XLP (consumer staples). XLP should perform better than XLY (consumer discretionary) during a recession as those products are the necessities.

Technical indicators such as SMA-50 (Simple Moving Average for the last 50 sessions), SMA-200 and RSI(14) are obtained from Finviz.com and the rest are obtained from Yahoo!Finance.com. After you buy the ETF, use a stop loss to protect your investment. For example, bio tech sector moved up for many months until it crashed in 2015. Change the stop loss value every month to protect your gains in this case.

As of 2/5/2016	SPY	XLP (staples)	XLY (discret.)
Price	190	50	71
NAV	192	50	73
• Technical			
SMA-50	-4%	0%	-7%
SMA-200	-6%	2%	-7%
RSI(14)	44	50	36
Other	Double bottom at $186		
• Fundamental			
P/E	17	20	19
Yield	2.1%	2.5%	1.5%
YTD return	-5%	0.5%	-5%
Net asset	174 B	9 B	10 B

Explanation

- The figures may not be identical among web sites due to the dates they are using.
- XLY has best discount among the 3 ETFs as most investors believe a recession is coming.
- XLP has less down trend among the 3 ETFs as expected.
- XLY is more undersold among the three as expected.
- Double bottom is a technical pattern that indicates the stock would surge upward.
- SPY has a better value according to its P/E.
- XLY's dividend is the least among the three as they have more tech companies in the ETF. They have to plow back the profits to research and development.
- XLP has the best YTD return among the three.
- As long as the asset is above 500 M (200 M for specialized ETFs), it is fine and all three pass this mark.

There are many metrics such as Debt/Equity not readily available from most web sites. Many sites list the top holdings of a specific ETF. Just average the metrics of the top ten or so of its stock holdings.

An example

This example evaluates RING, a gold miner, using ETFdb and Finviz that are free from the web. The data is from July, 6, 2020.

Bring up ETFdb and enter RING in the search. There are basic info that are important to me: Sector (gold miners), Asset Size (Large-Cap), Issuer (iShares), Inception (Jan. 31, 2012), Expense Ratio (0.39%) and Tax Form (1099).

They fit all my requirements. The expense ratio is higher than most ETFs that simulating an index such as SPY. I try to trade ETFs using Tax Form 1099 in my taxable accounts. The large cap created about 8 years ago by a reputable company are good.

Select "Dividend and Valuation". P/E of 17.39 is fine in a rank of 11 in 27 in similar group of ETFs. As in my books, I stated it is hard to evaluate miners. I buy this ETF primarily to fight the possibility of inflation and the potential depreciation of USD. The dividend rate of 0.52% (0.70% from Finviz) is in the low range of the scale; it is fine for me as dividend is not my concern.

There are more info from this web site. For simplicity, bring up Finviz:
- The short-term trend is up (SMA-20% = 8% and SMA-50% = 7%).
- The long-term trend is up (SMA-200% = 26%).
- It is close to overbought (RSI(14) = 64%; 65% to me is overbought).
- It is -4% from 52-w High. It has performed well from the YTD, Last Year, Last Quarter, Last Month and Last Week.
- It almost doubles in price from mid March this year.
- Avg. Vol. is fine.

From ETFdb, check the Holding. It has 39 stocks, so it is quite diversified for this industry. The two top holdings are NEM (19%) and ABX (18%), which is listed as GOLD in NYSX. I also consider to buy these two stocks in addition to RING. You can estimate the other metrics that are not available by averaging these two stocks. Here is my summary:

STOCK	NEM	GOLD
Forward P/E	20	25
Debt / Share	0.31	0.24
ROE	17%	22%
Sales Q/Q	43%	30%
EPS Q/Q	389%	254%
SMA50	2%	4%
RSI(14)	59%	60%
Insider Trans	-13%	N/A
Fidelity's Equity Summary Score	6.1	6.8

3 Rotate four ETFs

We can beat the market by rotating one ETF that represents the market such as SPY and cash via market timing.

During a market uptrend, rotating the following four ETFs could be more profitable than staying with SPY (or any ETF that simulating the market). Be warned that a short-term capital gain in taxable accounts is not treated as favorably as the long-term capital gain; check current tax laws.

The allocation percentages depend on your individual risk tolerance. You can use indexed mutual funds. Compare their expenses and restrictions. Some mutual funds charge you if you withdraw within a specific time period.

Select the best performer of last month (from Seeking Alpha, cnnFn, or one of many ETF/mutual fund sites). Add a contra ETF such as SH to take advantage of a falling market for more aggressive investors. Add sector ETFs to the described four ETFs such as XLY, XLP, XLE, XLF, XLU, IYW, XHB, IYM, OIL and XLU to expand your selection.

ETFs	Money Market	U.S.	International	Bond
Fidelity		Spartan Total Market	Spartan Global Market	Spartan US Bond
Vanguard		Total Stock Market	Total International Market	Total Bond Market
My choice	Fidelity	SPY	Vanguard	Fidelity
Suggest %				
During Market plunge	90%	0%	0%	10%
After plunge	10%	60%	20%	10%

Explanation

- The above are suggestions only. If your broker offers similar ETFs, consider using them.

- Check out any restrictions of the ETFs and commissions.
- 4 ETFs (one actually is a money market fund) are enough for most starters. They are diversified, low-cost and you do not need rebalancing except during a market plunge.
- The percentages are suggestions only. If you are less risk tolerant, allocate more to a money market fund, CD and/or bond ETF.
- Have at least 10% allocated to the money market fund for safety.
- When the market is risky, reduce stock equities (i.e. increase money market and bond allocations).
- The symbols for Fidelity ETFs are FSTMX, FSGDX and FBIDX.
- The symbols for Vanguard ETFs are VTSMX, VGTSX and VBMFX.
- If you are more advanced, use additional sector ETFs to rotate. Also buy long-term bond funds (such as 30-year Treasury) when the interest rates is 10% or more.

4   Simplest way to evaluate stocks

Beginners should trade ETFs only. This chapter is for the readers who are ready or getting ready to trade stocks. In general, ETFs are diversified, less volatile than trading stocks. However, stocks offer higher profit but higher risk.

Many stock researches have already been done recently and some are available free of charge. I have no affiliation with Fidelity except I retired from it. You can open an account with them with no balance. Their Equity Summary Score is one of the best indicators; I check out **value** stocks with score higher than 8. Concentrate on fundamental metrics such as P/E for long-term holds, and momentum metrics for short-term holds. Add criteria to limit the number of screened stocks. Finviz.com is a free screener.

Several sources

The popular ones are Morningstar, Value Line, The Street and Zacks (currently free for rankings of individual stocks). If they are not free, check out whether they are available from your local library. I have 3 simple ways to evaluate stocks starting with the simplest. In addition, read the articles on the selected stocks from Fidelity, Finviz, Seeking Alpha and many other sources for further evaluation.

Fidelity

Select only stocks that have Fidelity's Equity Summary Score 8 or higher. There are tons of information about a stock. Once a while I did not agree with the score such as SHOP and ZM that scored high in August, 2020. Include the following for your analysis.

A modified stock selection based on a magazine article

Most metrics are available from Finviz except EV/EBITDA.

1. Forward P/E (expected earnings and not based on the last twelve months). It should range from 5 to 15 (10 to 25 for high tech stocks). EV/EBITDA (from Yahoo!Finance) is a better choice as it includes the debts and cash than P/E; it would be more effective if it uses forward earnings. If you do not use EV/EBITDA, ensure Debt/Equity is less than 0.5 except for the debt-intensive industries.

2. ROE (Return of Equity) measures how well the company uses the capital. I prefer stocks with ROE greater than 5%.
3. Volatility. Conservative investors should select stocks with a beta of less than one (i.e. less volatile).
4. Insider Transactions for sales (i.e. negative) from should be less than 5%. If it is -5%, most likely the insiders are dumping it.
5. Compare the metrics such as P/E and Debt/Equity to its five-year average and its competitors (available in Fidelity).
6. Momentum. Check out the SMA-50 (actually SMA-50%) and SMA-200. Ideally they should be positive. SMA-50% is especially important for stocks you do not want to keep for a long time.
7. Check out articles on the stock as some recent events (for example a new lawsuit) have not been included in the metrics.
8. Compare the trend of the sector this stock is in. Under Finviz, enter the related sector ETF.

Summary

The sources are Fidelity (Equity Summary Score and various comparisons), Finviz and Yahoo!Finance (for EV/EBITDA). Value stocks should be held longer.

Category	Score / Metric	Value /Momentum
Score	Fidelity's Equity Summary Score	Both
Value	EV/EBITDA	Value
	P/E cheaper compared to 5-year avg.	Value
	P/E cheaper compared to its sector.	Value
	Insider Purchases	Both
Safety	Debt/Equity	Value
	Compare it to its sector.	Value
Momentum	50-SMA%	Momentum
	200-SMA% (for long term holds).	Value
Articles	Check out latest events	Both
Market	No purchase if market is risky.	Momentum

A simple scoring system using Finviz
Bring up Finviz.com and then enter the stock symbol.

No.	Metric	Good	Bad	Score
1	Forward P/E[1]	Between 2.5 and 12.5, Score = 2 < 12, Score = 1	> 50 or < 0, Score = -1	
2	P/ FCF[1]		>30 or < 0, Score = -1	
3	P/S[1]	< 0.8, Score = 1	< 0, Score = -1	
4	P/ B[1]	< 1, Score = 1	< 0, Score = -1	
5	Compare quarter to quarter of last year Sales Q/Q	> 15%, Score = 1	< 0, Score = -1	
6	EPS Q/Q	> 20%, Score = 1	< 0, Score = -1	
			Grand Score	
	Stock Symbol Date[2]	Current Price	SPY	

Footnote

[1] Negative values for Sales (due to accounting adjustments), Equity and Book are possible but not likely.

[2] The last row is for your information only. SPY is used to measure whether it will beat the market by comparing the return of this stock to the return of SPY.

The Score
Score each metric and sum up all the scores giving the Grand Score. If the Grand Score is 3, the stock passes this scoring system. Even if it is a 2, it still deserves further analysis if you have time. You may want to add scores from other vendors. To illustrate on using Fidelity, add 1 to the score if Fidelity's Equity Summary score is 8 or higher. Monitor the performance after every 6 months or so to see whether this scoring system beats the market.

Very basic advice for beginners
Beginners should stick with U.S. stocks with Market Cap greater than 800 M (million), Debt/Equity less than .25 (25%) except for debt-intensive industries such as utilities and airlines and Forward P/E between 5 to 20 (25 for high-tech companies). These metrics are all available from Finviz.com, which is free.

Do not have more than 20% of your portfolio in one stock (unless it is an ETF or mutual fund) and do not have more than 30% of your portfolio in one sector.

For more conservative investors, buy non-volatile stocks whose beta (available from Yahoo!Finance) is less than 1. Beta of 1 represents the market (the S&P 500 index). For example, a stock with beta 1.5 statistically fluctuates more than 50% of the market and hence it is very volatile.

Try paper trading to check out your strategy and your skill in trading stocks. If your broker does not provide one, use a spreadsheet to record your trades or check the availability of simulator.investopedia.com.

5 Simplest technical analysis

When the stock, the sector that the stock is in and the market are all above its SMA-N averages (Single Moving Average for the last N sessions), most likely the stock is trending up.

1. Bring up Finviz.com from your browser.

2. Enter SPY. Write down the SMA-200 (Single Moving Average for 200 sessions). Positive numbers indicate that the trend for the market is up.

   However, the market could be peaking or overbought. Be careful when SMA-200 is over 5% and / or RSI(14) is over 65%. RSI is a metric on over bought / under bought.

3. Enter the sector ETF the stock is in. Write down the SMA-50. Positive numbers indicate that trend for the sector is up.

   However, the sector could be peaking or overbought. Be careful when the SMA-200 is over 10% and / or RSI(14) is over 65%.

4. Enter the stock symbol. If your average holding period of the stocks is 200, use SMA-200 and so on. I recommend SMA-200 for holding value stocks long term and SMA-50 for momentum stocks. Write down the SMA-N for your stock. Positive numbers indicate that the trend is up.

   However, the stock could be peaking or overbought. Be careful when the SMA-200 (or SMA-50) is over 25% and / or RSI(14) is over 65%.

If the above three criteria and the fundamental criteria are satisfied, most likely it is a good buy. If you buy sector ETFs or mutual funds only, you can skip step #4. In any case, use stop loss to protect your investment.

6 Summary

The following improves the odds of success but there is no guarantee.

Risky Market?

Bring up Finviz.com. Enter SPY. If both SMA-50% and SMA-200% are both negative, do not invest especially when SMA-50% is more negative than SMA-200%.

Evaluate value stocks from others' research
Gather a list of stocks from screens and/or recommendations from magazines. Use researches that are available. Value stocks should be kept for at least 6 months and do another evaluation then. There are many other free sources such as IBD, GuruFocus, Zacks and Morningstar.

Name	Pass Grade	Link[1]
Vector Vest[2]	VST > 1 and RV > 1	Link
Value Line[3]	Timeliness > Average	
	Proj. 3-5 yr.% > 5%	
Fidelity Equity Summary Score	>5	Customer

1   Links. Just Google the Name and select the web site. Some may no longer be free.
2   Free for limited number of stocks and free trial.
3   Should be available from your local library.

Evaluate stocks
Bring up Finviz.com and enter the stock symbol.

Metric	Passing Grade
Forward P/E	Between 5 and 15
P/FCF	< 15 and ratio is positive
Sales Q/Q	>10
EPS Q/Q	>15

Intangible Analysis
Bring up Finviz, Fidellity or Seeking Alpha and enter the stock symbol. To prevent manipulation, only use it for stocks with larger cap (> 200 M) and higher daily average volume (> 10,000 shares).

Section III: Find and evaluate stocks

1 Where the web sites are

- **Free and simple screen sites**

    They are described in this article or type the following
    http://stocks.about.com/od/researchtools/a/071909screenlist.htm

    - Yahoo!Finance.
      Click here or type
      http://screener.finance.yahoo.com/stocks.html

    - Finviz.
      Click here or type
      http://Finviz.com/screener.ashx

      How to scan using Finviz (YouTube).
      https://www.YouTube.com/watch?v=aQ_0FTg9Cfw

      Screening using technical indicators   (particularly useful for momentum stocks).
      https://www.YouTube.com/watch?v=RZRP2NeSX0s

    - Your broker.
      Fidelity's screens are more sophisticated than most.

    - More options: Google, CNBC.com and Moringstar.com.

    Here is a list.
    http://stocks.about.com/od/researchtools/a/071909screenlist.htm

- **Sophisticated screens (usually not free)**

    Most of them are more complicated and need time to learn. Both Vector Vest and Stock123 provide historical databases for back testing your screens. Zacks has an earnings revision database at extra cost. GuruFocus has an easy-to-use but powerful screen function.

AAII provides screened stocks from various screens in its low-priced subscription. Both AAII and Value Line take care of some specific industries, but they provide no historical database at least for regular subscriptions. AAII provides historical performance summaries of their screens included in its subscription.

Afterthoughts

Here are the links to screens provided by Marketwatch and NASDAQ.
http://www.marketwatch.com/tools/stockre...
http://www.nasdaq.com/reference/stock-sc...

How to find quality stocks.
http://seekingalpha.com/article/2381395-how-to-identify-quality-stocks-and-is-there-really-alpha-to-be-had

Filler
"Sell in May" could be a self-fulfilled prophecy. I prefer to sell on April 1 and come back on Oct. 15 to avoid the herd.

NASDAQ

It is quite similar to GuruFocus's screens in some aspects, but quite simplified. Currently it is free. Bring up Nasqaq.com from your browser. Select "Investing" and then "Guru Screeners".

The following is an illustration on 6/9/2016. Select "P/E Growth Investors" and change "Some" to "Strong". Click on "Go".

I had 5 stocks with "Strong": THO, MPX, GGAL (ADR), BRDCY (ADR) and BMA (ADR). If you prefer U.S. companies only, you only have THO and MPX and both had a desirable "Proj. P/E" under 20.

Alternatively to reduce the number of screened stocks, include stocks with "Some Strong". Sort the "Proj. P/E" in ascending order. If it is blank, most likely it is losing money or there is no estimate for this stock. Use Finviz.com or Yahoo!Finance to confirm.

PEG (P/E growth) is a growth metric and it is available for sorting. You need to evaluate each screened stock. For example, a low P/E stock may not be good if it has excessive debt, or serious pending lawsuits.

Click on the stock THO. It explains how Peter and other gurus score this stock. If you use 70% as a passing grade, 7 gurus rate it a pass and 3 gurus rated it failed.

Click on "Detailed Analysis". Peter rates 4 "Pass" and 2 "Neutral" together with the description.

Fidelity

Fidelity offers a strong screen function. The most unique feature is incorporating its Equity Summary Score (used to be Analyst's Opinion) and some outside researches such as Zacks and Ford.

From the main menu, select "News and Research", "Screen and Filter" and then "Start a screen".

The following example selects stocks with the following criteria: Security Price (2 to 250), Market Cap. (300 and above), Equity Summary Score (8 and above), Zacks (Strongest) and Ford (Strongest). It displays the 10 stocks. Research each stock. Read the News about each stock. You may want to use Finviz.com, Yahoo!Finance and other sources to double check.

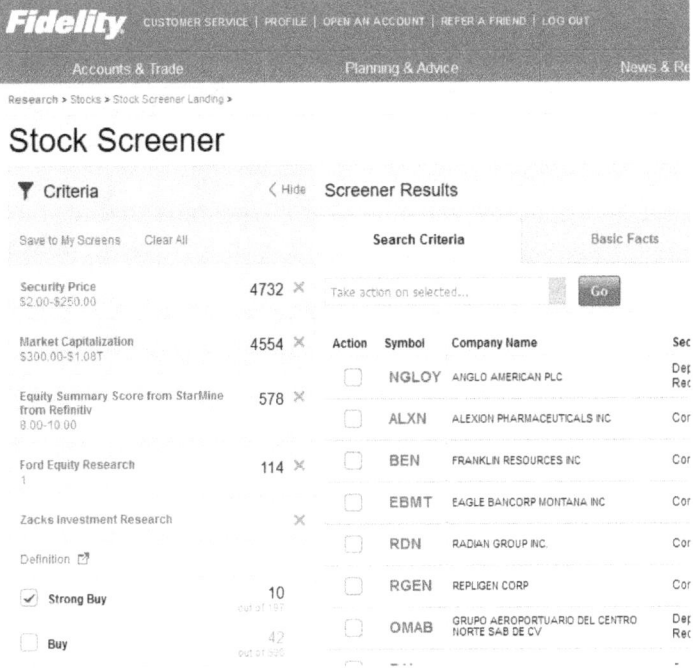

The following describes some of the features.

- Equity Summary Score. It is one of the major metrics I use in my proprietary scoring systems. They are not available to many small stocks. From my limited database in 7/2015 and for short durations, the results are:

Short Term: (7% return for the average)

Metric	Parm. 1	No. of Stocks	%	Parm. 2	No.	%	Predictability
Fidelity Analyst	Buy	150	10%	Sell	279	3%	Good

Long Term: (8% return for the average)

Metric	Parm. 1	No. of Stocks	%	Parm. 2	No.	%	Predictability
Fidelity Analyst	Buy	90	17%	Sell	208	4%	Good

It has its own limits, but they are very minor to me.

First, it does not have a historical database for verifying the screen performance such as the return after a year. However, I do not know any site that provides this function free. To work around this, I save the results in a spread sheet and update the performance.

Secondly, it does not provide many other filter criteria that can be found in other systems such as technical indicators or insider transactions found in Finviz.com. I use other sites for further evaluation.

Most investors should find that this screening is a very good tool and very easy to use.

2 Finviz.com screener

You should use fundamental metrics for fundamental stocks, growth metrics for growth stocks, momentum metrics for momentum stocks, or a combination. Basically you want to keep the fundamental stocks longer so the market would realize their values.

Finviz.com provides a screening function incorporating both fundamental and technical metrics and is one of the best free sites. Bring up Finviz.com in your browser and select screener. You have 4 tabs: Descriptive, Fundamental, Technical and All. It has the following features:

- The criteria specified can be saved but the number is limited.
- The searched stocks can be saved in a portfolio (for paper trading and performance monitoring).
- Technical indicators.
- For an extra fee, you can have a historical database. This would help you to test your strategies. The historical database is quite limited for some technical parameters only.
- Some advanced technical indicators work well especially useful in momentum trading.
- Use technical patterns. My favorites are Head and Shoulder and Double Bottoms (Peaks).
- Combine fundamental metrics and technical metrics to narrow down your selection.
- Combine fundamental metrics and technical metrics to narrow down your selection.
- Add Insider Trans (> 5% for me), Short Squeeze (> 20%), etc. for specific purposes.
- Candlesticks is hard to master. You need to read a book dedicated to it.

http://www.investopedia.com/terms/c/candlestick.asp
https://www.youtube.com/watch?v=FsqoV1aVrUc&list=WL&index=56

Finviz's screener lacks the following features:

- Stocks with prices trending up in the last several weeks (such as increasing X% in the previous week).

- Using exponential moving averages that supposedly have better predictive power than simple moving averages for momentum investing.
- Selecting ranges such as selecting all three major exchanges and market cap ranges.
- P/E for an ETF. It can be obtained from other sources such as ETFdb.com.
- When the earnings (E) is negative, you may have the wrong values for P/E and the metrics using E. For example, if you want stocks with P/E less than 20, the screener returns you stocks with negative earnings.
- Combine fundamental metrics and technical metrics to narrow down your selection.

All of these missing features can be worked around. The paid version may provide better functions.

Links:

Investopedia.
http://www.investopedia.com/university/features-of-Finviz-elite/other-chart-features.asp

How to scan using Finviz (YouTube).
https://www.YouTube.com/watch?v=aQ_0FTg9Cfw
https://www.youtube.com/watch?v=tHtovnCY6uY&list=WL&index=96
(Recommended)

Finviz's screener tutorial.
https://www.youtube.com/watch?v=glMtwB7OVf4&list=WL&index=56

Swing trading
https://www.youtube.com/watch?v=M8sNMhPJINU&list=WL&index=55

Screening using technical indicators (YouTube).
https://www.YouTube.com/watch?v=RZRP2NeSX0s

A screener example

The following is an example. Fine tune the selection criteria according to your personal criteria and risk tolerance.

- Bring up Finviz.com from your browser. Select Screener, the third tab. As of 3/24/2015, we have 7066 stocks.

- For illustration purposes, we would like to find stocks with double bottoms, a positive technical indicator. Select the Technical tab. Select Pattern and then Double Bottom. Now we have 257 stocks.

- Select the Fundamental tab that is next to the Technical tab. Select Forward P/E and then select "under 20". Now, we have 86 stocks.

- Select Debt/Equity less than .5. Now, we have 45 stocks. Some industries such as utilities are traditionally high in debt, so you can use 'less than 1'.

- Select EPS growth Q-to-Q over 10%. Now, we have 19 stocks.

- Select the Description tab. Select Country to USA. Now, we have 17 stocks.

- Select Price > 1. Select Avg. Volume "Over 100K". Select Float Short "Under 10%. Select Analyst Recs. "Buy or better". Now we have 9 stocks.

  Now we can evaluate them one by one using Fundamental Analysis, Intangible Analysis, Qualitative Analysis and Technical Analysis. The purpose of screening is to filter the 7000 stocks to a small number (9 stocks in this case).

Skip the stocks that have the Earnings Date within 2 weeks. If you already have too many stocks in the same industry, skip that stock. You can save the screen when you have registered with Finviz.com. It is free. Check the performance of your selections after 3 months or so.

Other sources

Paper trade and check the actual performance before investing your money. Many popular screens provided by many sites worked before but may not work now. It could be too many folks using the same strategy. Hence it is important to check the current performances of the screen you are using. For yardstick, use SPY or similar ETF that simulates the market. Here are some sources beside Finviz.com.

Your broker

Most broker sites have screen functions. Some have screens to simulate what a specific guru such as what Warren Buffett would buy.

IBD (a subscription service)

From my check on the IBD 50, they're good in the last 10 years, but not that good in the last 5 years – the victim of their own success? They provide stocks from their screens. Most screens are for momentum stocks and large caps. Here are the updated days for specific lists as of this writing.

Stocks Group	Published
Sector Leaders	Daily
Stock spotlight	Daily
Top World	Daily
IBD 50	Mon. and Wed.
Weekly Review	Fri.
Big Cap 20	Tue.

You may want to check out individual stocks with Stock Checkup and then analyze them again. The following are good parameters: Composite Rating, Industry Ranking (finer and better than Sector Ranking) and Relative Price. Understand their parameters and apply accordingly - the same for most other vendors.

IBD prefers large and growing companies with institutional ownership. Some of their parameters may not make sense for small, value and/or turn around companies.

Common parameters

Different styles of investing use different parameters for screening stocks. Here is my suggested parameters in using Finviz.com. Vary them to your risk tolerance and market conditions. Finviz.com is not complete in all functions, but it could the best free screener that incorporates both the fundamental and the technical criteria. The first table is for Value and the next one for Growth. The last one is for finding stocks that the institutional investors are trading.

Screening value stocks

Value Screens	Common	Penny	Micro Cap	Dividend
General				
Market Cap (M)	>500 M	<50 M	50-200 M	+Mid(>2B)
Price	>5	<5	1-15	>5
In all 3 Exchanges	In	Not In	Most are In	In
Avg. Volume	>100K	>5K	>10K	>100K
Country	USA	USA	USA	USA
Dividend%				>3%
Float Short	<10%	<10%	<10%	<10%
Analyst Rec	Buy or +	Buy or + if avail.	Buy or +	Buy or +
Fundamental				
Forward P/E	<20	<20	<20	<25
ROE	>10	>10	>5	>15
QQ earning	>0			>0
QQ sales	>0			>0
PEG	<1	<1	<1	<1.2
Payout%				20-50%
P/S	<10	<10	<10	<10
Technical				
Price above 200 SMA	Yes	Yes	Yes	Yes
RSI(14)	<70	<70	<70	<70

There may be no analysts or very few following penny stocks and micro-cap stocks. QQ is quarter to quarter.

Screening Growth Stocks

Growth Screen	Common	Technical	Momentum
General			
Market Cap (M)	>50	> 1,000	>500
Price	>1	>10	>5
Exchanges (Major 3)	In	In	In
Avg. Volume	>50K	>200K	>100K
Fundamental			
Forward P/E	<30	<30	<30
Return of Equity	>5	>0	>0
QQ earning	>10%	>15%	>20%
QQ sales	>5%	> 5%	>10%
PEG	<1	<1	<1
Analyst recs.	Buy or +		
Technical			
Price above 200 SMA	Yes	Yes	
50 SMA	Yes	Yes	Yes
RSI	< 75	< 75	

Short-term trends are important for momentum stocks.

Explanation

The above are suggestions only. Adjust them to your personal preferences and risk tolerance.

- Finviz screener lacks ranges, such as market cap and multiple of exchanges. Most Finviz's parameters do not have a range option such as Exchanges, so you need to run the screen three times, one for each of the three major exchanges.

- Average Volume. When the price of the stock is less than $3, double the average volume requirement. In most cases, 10K is quite acceptable to me. When the volume is small, you may have to pay more (a.k.a. spread) to trade.

- There are many fundamental metrics such as Debt/Equity and Price/Free Cash Flow that are not included here, but they should be included in your further evaluation. Each industry sector has different thresholds. For example, the P/S is very different for a supermarket rather than a high-tech company. Compare the company to the average value of the companies in the same sector. Many sites including GuruFocus.com and Fidelity.com have the average values displayed.

- For momentum stock, you can ignore most of the fundamentals and concentrate on the price trend such as SMA-20% (Simple Moving Average for the last 20 trade sessions) and SMA-50%. The higher the percent, the higher it is away from its own average. You do not want to hold momentum stocks too long (max. 3 months unless the momentum is still uptrend); personally my max. is 1 month.

- For growth stocks, ensure the PEG (P/E growth), quarter-to-quarter earnings and quarter-to-quarter sales are above the averages in its own sector and/or the market.

- Technical analysis favors large cap stocks with large volumes. I prefer stocks with positive earnings and they are fundamentally sound.

- When the SMA-20%, SMA-50% and SMA-200% are all positive, they should be in an uptrend.
- RSI(14) indicates whether the stock is oversold (>65) or under bought (<30). The range is my suggestion only.
- You may want to check out your strategies using a virtual account from your broker.

A general guideline for Institutional investors

Criteria	Value
Description	
Relative Volume	Over 2 M
Country	USA usually
Institution Ownership	Over 50%
Technical	
SMA-200	>10%
Volatility	Week – Over 3%
RSI(14)	>40%
Fundamental	
Market Cap	>1B
ROE	>10%

- Again, these are my suggested metrics. I prefer USA companies and many are global companies. If you use foreign countries, ensure they are larger companies and/or in countries that have regulations similar to our SEC's.
- For value investors, select Forward P/E less than 20 (25 for high-tech companies) and their Earnings are positive.
- Check out how many analysts are following the stocks that you are interested in.

To illustrate, I find 12 stocks. I narrow them down to 3. First, I skip all stocks that already have had more than 10% rise recently. They may have risen too high already.

Select profitable stocks with forward P/E less than 25. "Debt/Equity" is less than .5 (50%). Then, ROI is higher than 25%. Stop when you have reached the optimal number of stocks (3 for me in this example).

If you find too many stocks, tighten the criteria and vice versa. Save the criteria and the selected stocks in a portfolio for paper trading.

Filler: Irresponsible is my best defense

I told my date that I would not be responsible after the second drink due to the lack of an enzyme.

Filler

Starbucks is being sued for too many ice cubes in the ice coffee. If he wins, he would sue MacDonald's, Burger King... and be a billionaire. Why did I not think of this? The lady won for the spilling of hot coffee. The jury did not know that eventually we had to pay for all of these and made the lawyers rich. Too many unproductive lawyers makes it tough to operate a business including small businesses. In many countries besides the U.S., the one who sues and loses has to pay for court expenses.

3   Finviz parameters

Most metrics are described in Finviz (via Help), Investopedia and/or Wikipedia and my chapter on P/E. The following are my personal comments and why I feel some metrics are more important than others. Compare the ratios to the companies in the same sector and also its averages from the last 5 years.

From your browser, enter Finviz.com. Enter a symbol (I used ABEO for discussion). A chart is displayed with the prices and volumes for the last nine months. SMAs (Single Moving Average) are displayed sometimes with other technical indicators. Intraday, Daily and Weekly options are available.

Besides the metrics described next and the chart, it describes what the company does, analysts' recommendations (I prefer Fidelity's Equity Summary), insiders' trading and articles that are good for qualitative analysis. "Financial Highlights and Statements" are materials for more in-depth analysis and they were more important decades ago when most financial ratios had not been calculated for you.

The following metrics are roughly based on the flow of Finviz from top to bottom and left to right. I skip those metrics that I believe are not too important. You can also place your cursor on the metric to have the description from Finviz. Some metrics are left blank to indicate they are not applicable (zero, negative or not available). For example, the Debt/Equity of YRCW in 1/2019 is blank (same as null) due to Equity being negative. From Yahoo!Finance, it has a total debt of 888M.

- **Index**. Most of us trade stocks in the three major exchanges in the USA. Stocks listed in over-the-counter are too risky for most of us. Skip the stocks in local exchanges and foreign exchanges if you are not an expert on these stocks. I screen the stocks and then ignore the stocks that are not in the Dow, NASDAC and Amex. Other screeners may let you to select a group of exchanges.

- **Market Cap** (MC). To me, stocks below 50M are risky even they could be very profitable. Ensure the Avg. Volume is at least 10,000 shares and / or your order is less than 1% of the average volume. Some small stocks are controlled by the owners and have small volumes. In this case you cannot sell your stock easily.

Float = Outstanding shares – Insider shares.

Usually it does not matter as they are typically the same. However, it does for small companies with large insider shares. Most of these owners do not want to sell their family businesses and hence they reduce the chance of being acquired entirely or partially for good prices.

- If **Forward P/E** (a.k.a. Expected P/E) is not provided, use the P/E which is based on the trailing last 12 months (TTM). Alternatively, calculate the E by using the E from P/E and multiplying it by its growth rate. It may not be seasonally adjusted. I prefer Expected P/E (or called Forward P/E) as it provides a better predictability power from my limited research.

  Finviz.com leaves the P/E blank (same as null) if the earnings are negative. In this case, I would check out Yahoo!Finance's EV / EBITDA, which also considers taxes and interests. It is similar to the blank on some metrics, if the Asset is negative even they seldom occur.

  Earnings Yield is equal to E/P and True Earnings Yield (my term) is EBITDA / EV. It is easier to understand. Compare it to the annual dividend yield of a 10-year Treasury which is quite safe. It is also useful in screening and sorting the screened stocks. If you use P/E instead of E/P, in most cases you need to screen or sort stocks with a clause "P/E > 0".

  Compare the P/E or Forward P/E with the average P/E for the sector and its average P/E for the last 5 years that are available from Fidelity.com. Some sectors have high P/Es. If the sector is cyclical, the earnings could be affected.

- **Cash / share**. It is used to calculate Pow P/E and Pow EY when EV/EBITDA is not available. To illustrate, if the stock is $10 and it has $10 cash / share without debt (i.e. Debt/Equity = 0), most likely it is underpriced as you can get the whole company for nothing. You should find out why the price is so low. It could be the market ignoring the stock, or there is a serious event happening such as major lawsuit.

- **Dividend %** is useful for income investors. The payout ratio should not be more than 30% except for matured companies.

- **Recs**. Select stocks with 1 or 2. Do not base your stock selection on this recommendation alone. There have been many bad recommendations that could cost you a fortune in losses. Use Fidelity's Equity Summary Score instead.

- **PEG** is a measure of the growth of P/E and hence a growth metric. The lower value is better as long as earnings are positive. If earnings are negative, then the reverse is true. It is a defect in using P/E and PEG and that's why I recommend EY (Earnings Yield) and EYG, earnings yield growth.

  If there are two companies with the same P/E, the one with a better PEG ratio is better. If two companies have the same E/P, the company with higher Earnings Growth (EPS Q/Q) would be better.

- **P/B**. Book value (= Total Assets − Total Liabilities) may not include intangible asset such as patents. Do not trust it 100%, so is ROE which is based on book value. Negative equity is possible when Total Liabilities is more than Total Assets.

- **P/S**. If two companies are unprofitable, this ratio can be used. I prefer profitable companies.

- **P/FCF**. I prefer it to be greater than 0 and less than 50 for value investors. Most metrics can be manipulated easily, but not this one.

- **Sales Q/Q** reduces the seasonal deviation. To illustrate, retail sales for the Christmas season should be compared it to the same season in prior year.

- **EPS Q/Q**. Same as above. I prefer the growth of EPS over Sales. Both of these Q/Q ratios are growth metrics. When a company terminates its unprofitable product(s), its Sales Q/Q could be down but its EPS Q/Q could be up. In 2000, many internet companies had great Sales Q/Qs but negative EPS Q/Qs.

  Q/Q comparison (quarter to quarter) takes out the seasonal variations.

When the company buys its own shares, EPS could be misleading as E is fixed and the number of shares is reduced. In most cases, the fundamentals of the company has not changed.

- Positive **Insider** Transactions are favorable. Sometimes, they are misleading. Need to scroll to the end of the screen and check out more info there. If the transactions are outdated such as 3 months or so ago, and or they are buys in a similar amount than the sells a while ago, they are not important. Insiders know the company better than us. So is Institutional Transactions as institutional investors move the market.

- Insider Own, Shares Outstanding and Shares **Float** determine the number of shares that are available for trading. A small Float with a high Insider Own limits trading and the stock should be avoided in most cases. Compare your trade position for the stock to the Avg. Volume.

- **Profit Margin**. I prefer it over Gross Margin and Oper. Margin which does not include interest expenses and taxes. When you sell software, the Gross Margin is high as it does not include development, support and marketing, etc. A retail store has low Gross Margin. It all depends on the industry, and hence it is better to compare companies in the same industry.

- **Short Float**. I prefer it to be less than 10%. If it is greater than 10%, the shorters could find something wrong with the company. If it is over 25%, I would check the fundamentals. If they are good, I would buy expecting a short squeeze potential. It has been risky but proven to be profitable for me.

- Technical metrics: SMA-20, SMA-50 and SMA-200. Finviz expresses them in convenient percentages. If they are all positive, it means the trend is up. SMA-20 is short-term trend and SMA-200 is a long-term trend. If you are short-term swing investor, stick with short-term trend and vice versa. The first two are momentum grades. Many long-term investors do not buy stocks when their SMA-200% is negative.

- **RSI(14)**. If it greater than 65%, it is overbought. If it is under 30%, it is under bought for me. Some use 5% up or down than mine. Use it as a reference. Most stocks making new heights are always overbought, and many of these stocks keep on rising. I recommend use trailing stops to protect your profit.

- **Beta**. A volatile stock fluctuates a lot. It is good for short-term traders. A beta of 1 means the stock would fluctuate with the market and more volatile if it is higher than 1. For volatile stocks (higher than 1), the stops should be higher. For example, if your stops are normally 5%, you may want to use 7% or even higher.

- Management performance is measured by **ROE**. It is also judged by **Analysts' Rec.** and Institutional Ownership (except for small companies). The confidence of their own ability, the company and its sector is measured by Insider Ownership and Insider Purchases.

  ROE = Net Income / Average Shareholder's Equity
  According to Investopedia, a normal ROE for utilities should be 10% while high tech companies should be 15%. Compare this ration and many other ratios with its peers that is available from Fidelity.

- Avoid all bankrupting companies at all cost. Debt/Equity, P/FCF, Cash/Sh., P/B, Profit Margin, Forward P/E, Short Float, RSI(14), SMA20% and SMA50 would give us hints. Need to summarize all the info and study many other factors such as obsoleting products (including drugs).

- Unless you have concrete information, do not buy stocks a week or so before the Earnings Date.

More useful information:

- The price chart. It has a lot of features such as the resistance line. Some charts include technical indicators such as double top (a bearish warning) and double bottom (a bullish sign).
- Description under the symbol. It briefly describes what the company (sector and industry) does and its country of registration. You want to buy a stock within a sector that is trending up. For example according to Finviz, Apple is in the Consumer Goods sector and the Electronic Equipment industry.

  If you do not want to buy foreign stocks, skip it if it is not listed in the US exchange.
- Articles on the company for qualitative analysis.
- Insider trading. Pay more attention to the insider purchases at market prices. Use common sense.
- The last line lets you open Yahoo!Finance and other sites.

Your broker's web site

Your broker web site should have plenty of tools to analyze stocks. As of Dec., 2018, Fidelity lets you use their extensive research free by opening an account with no position restriction. I describe some of their metrics that should be beneficial to your research.

- Equity Summary Score. Potentially good buy when it is 7 (8 for conservative investors) or higher. With some exceptions, you should avoid or short stocks if the score is 3 or below. The stocks ranking from 4 to 6 could be turnaround candidates if they are supported by good Q/Q Earnings and/or good news.

- The 5-year averages are good yardsticks. For example, in Dec., 2018, C's P/E is about 9 and the average is 14. Hence it is a value buy.

Quick and dirty

Many times we need to evaluate a stock fast such as taking action due to some development. Refer to my other article "Simplest way to evaluate stocks". The following should take a few minutes. Bring up Finviz.com and enter the stock symbol.

Using SWKS on 6/10/16 to illustrate, Forward P/E is about 11 (fine between 3 and 25), Debt/Eq. is 0 (fine less than .5), ROE is 30% (fine greater than 5%) and P/PCF is 31 (fine if not negative).

Also, check out Market Cap, Avg. Volume, Dividend, Short Float (fine between 0% and 10%), Country and Industry. Judging from the above, it is a buy.

If you have more time, check out the following: Recom. (Ok if less than 2.5), P/B (fine between .5 and 4), Sales Q/Q (fine if not negative), EPS Q/Q (fine if not negative), Cash/Sh (compare it to Debt/Sh) and Profit Margin (fine >5%). Check some articles described for this stock.

5-minute stock evaluation

It takes even less time than the above "Quick and Dirty". However, I recommend you should spend more time in researching stocks.

- From Finviz.com, enter the stock or ETF symbol. Look at the number of reds in metrics. If there have more than greens, most likely it is not a good stock.

- It should be fine if Fidelity's Equity Summary Score is greater than 8.

If you have more time, I recommend you to check the following:

- Check out Forward P/E (E>0 and P/E < 20), Debut / Equity (< 50%) and P/FCF (not in red color).

    If time is allowed, replace Forward P/E with True P/E (same as "EV/EBITDA"), which is available from Yahoo!Finance and other sources.

- SMA20 (or SMA50 for longer holding period). If SMA20 is > 10%, it is trending up.

- It is fine if the Insider Transaction is positive.

- Be cautious on foreign stocks and low-volume stocks.

- If most of the above are positive, it is likely a buy. As in life, nothing is 100% certain.

Links
PEG: http://en.wikipedia.org/wiki/PEG_ratio
Short %: http://www.investopedia.com/university/shortselling/shortselling1.asp#axzz2LNDvpemo
Openinsider: http://www.openinsider.com/
Finviz: http://Finviz.com/
terms: http://www.Finviz.com/help/screener.ashx
Insider Cow: http://www.insidercow.com/
Current Ratio: http://en.wikipedia.org/wiki/Current_ratio
How to find quality stocks.
http://seekingalpha.com/article/2381395-how-to-identify-quality-stocks-and-is-there-really-alpha-to-be-had

Fidelity stock research

You have to be their customer to access all their research. If you are not one already, open an account with the minimal requirements (none as of this writing) and optionally buy a no-commission ETF from them. Their research is extensive and it could be the biggest bargain. Their StarMine (Analyst Opinions) has been proven to be a good predictor to me. Your broker other than Fidelity may provide similar tools.

The following describes some of the features.

- Analyst Opinion (now Equity Summary Score). It is one of the major metrics I use in my proprietary scoring systems. They do not track a lot of small stocks. From my limited database in 7/2015 and for short durations, the results are:

Short Term: (7% return for the average)

Metric	Parm. 1	No. of Stocks	%	Parm. 2	No.	%	Predicta-bility
Fidelity Analyst	Buy	150	10%	Sell	279	3%	Good

Long Term: (8% return for the average)

Metric	Parm. 1	No. of Stocks	%	Parm. 2	No.	%	Predicta-bility
Fidelity Analyst	Buy	90	17%	Sell	208	4%	Good

- ETP (ETF to me) evaluation.
- Key Statistics. Select the industry leader by comparing the metrics to its peers. They also compare their own metrics to the average of several years. The 5-year average of P/E is useful.
- Charts for technical analysis.

Research Reports and Financial Statements give us more information about the company.

Blue Chip Growth website is no longer free. It is easy to use Fidelity to replace their grades.

4   Common filters

These are my personal choice beside penny stocks. Adjust them to your preferences.

1. Traded in one of the three major exchanges, or specific exchange(s) for your country.

2. Market cap > 200 million.

3. Price > 2.

4. Average daily volume > 8,000 (6,000 if stock price > 200) shares.

The following are the secondary filters. Adjust them to your personal requirements.

1. Short % less than 15% (some use 10%).

2. Expected earning yield (E/P, reversal of P/E) > 5% and < 30%.

3. SMA (simple moving average) is positive for good entry point. Bottom fishers can skip this one as it will not find bottom prices.

    Buy the stock when the price is above the moving average.

    Moving average could be 20 days (trade sessions), 50 days and 200 days, or any days you specify.

    Choose it according to your holding period of a stock. If you hold your stock usually for 90 days, use the 90-day SMA.

Ensure positive earnings in using P/E (by specifying E > 0) or use E/P instead if available. Sorting on P/E will not be in the right order as intended for stocks with negative earnings.

If you only want to deal with large companies, use Market Cap > 1 billion (many use 10 B) and Price > 10 (many exceptions for price).

Small stocks (with prices between $1 and $2 and market caps between 100M to 300M) may have the best performances but at higher risk. Most analysts and institutional investors do not consider them, so a thorough analysis could find some gems.

There are many exceptions. At one time ALU was a $1 stock but it had a market cap of 2 B.

Do not trade stocks with minimal volume as the spread (between ask price and bid price) is high. Expect to pay more for their trades. I traded one stock with the owner and his family as the major stock owners. It took me a long time to sell this stock at a far lower price than I asked for.

The number of shares traded is a very rough estimate to determine the daily average volume. The correct calculation is the ratio of No. of Shares of your order / Average Daily Volume to adjust for the price difference (a small stock price has higher volume logically). You can buy the stock easier when this ratio is 1% than the ratio of 50% for example.

---

5   Sectors to be cautious with

There are many reasons to be very cautious when investing in the following sectors. However, Technical Analysis (a.k.a. charting) would give you more hints than the fundamentals for stocks for these sectors. If the big guys are dumping, most likely Technical Analysis (or the simplest SMA-20) would tell you that.

Loan companies/banks
The financial statements do not show the quality of their loan portfolios. Following this advice, you may be able to skip the banks that melted down in 2007. The peak of Citigroup is $550 and several banks went bankrupt.

Many metrics are not relevant for banks such as Debt/Equity and EBIT. The rising <u>interest rate</u> would be good for banks' profits.

Drug (generic is ok)

Understanding the complexities of the drug pipelines, its potential profits for new drugs and the expiration of the current drugs may not worth the effort for most retail investors. In addition, a serious lawsuit and / or a serious problem with a drug could wipe out a good percentage of the stock price. When a drug shows unpromising sign(s) in any trial phase, the stock could plunge and vice versa.

Miners

It is extremely difficult to estimate how much ore (sometimes a miner owns several different types of ores and/or of different grades in the same or different mines) that a company has. It is further complicated by the complexities to extract and transport them. When the total of these costs is greater than its production price, the company will not be profitable. Understanding the market for ore futures is another discipline.

Many mining companies are in foreign countries such as Canada, Australia and countries in South America. Their financial statements of Canada and Australia are more trustworthy than most other emerging countries.

One potential problem of mining companies from many emerging countries is nationalization.

Mining rare earth ore is extremely risky when the profit depends on how China, a major producer of these ores, will price these ores. After China announced the export restrictions on rare earth elements, several non-Chinese companies announced to reopen their mines for rare earths, but few have made any profits as of 2013. Developed countries have stricter environmental regulations.

Coal and eventually oil suffer from the rising use of cleaner energy such as solar and wind.

Insurance companies

Insurance companies profit by:

1. The difference between the total premiums received and the total claims minus expenses in running the company.

2. How well they invest the premiums; you pay your premiums earlier than you may collect from any claims.

They can protect the profits in #1 by restricting claims by natural disasters such as earthquakes and by re-insuring. However, a bad disaster could wipe out a lot of their profits.

Even if the insurance company shows you its investment portfolio, most of us, the retail investors, do not have the time and expertise to analyze it.

Emerging countries (not a sector)

Their financial statements especially from small companies cannot be trusted, and many countries use different accounting standards. Emerging countries are where the economic growth is. I trade FXI, an ETF, rather than individual Chinese companies. I have lost a lot in small Chinese companies due to frauds and politics. To check out whether the stock is an ADR, try ADR.COM (https://www.adr.com/).

Stocks with low volumes (not a sector)

Most likely you pay a high spread to trade these stocks. They can be manipulated easier. I had a hard time trying to sell a stock owned by a few owners.

For simplicity, I trade stocks with the average daily trade volume over 6,000 shares (double it if the price is $2 or less). A better way could be by calculating the percent of your trade quantity / average daily trade volume; it would reduce the effect of penny stocks that have larger volumes due to the low prices.

Good business and bad business

Banking is a good business in a growing economy. My deposit in them makes virtually zero interest, and they loan the same money making 3%. If they are more cautious in loaning, they should make good profits.

Restaurant is an easy business to run, but it is very hard to make good money. With the rising of minimal wages, it will get even tougher. That could be the reason for so many coupons today. The high-end restaurants are doing better due to the rising stock market. The pandemic of 2020 would wipe out a lot of small restaurants.

Retailing is a tough business. Look at the top 10 retailers 15 years ago, I can only find two including Macy's that are still surviving. Most are either went bankrupt or being acquired. Even Macy's was not in good financial shape. Amazon is the killer.

Airlines are a tough business. You can tell by the average increase in fares in the last 10 years. It cannot even beat inflation. They have to charge you for everything. The next frontier charge is the rest room (especially for long-distance flights). Now I understand why they call themselves "Frontier Air". As of 2014, it is quite profitable due to mergers and lower fuel cost. The pandemic of 2020 may be the toughest time for airlines. As of 5/2020, Boeing has many serious troubles and they can only survive with a bailout from the government.

There are several software companies that produce software such as the virus detecting programs and tax preparation software. The customers faithfully buy new versions every year. That's great business.

Afterthoughts

As of 8/2013, is the emerging market oversold?
http://seekingalpha.com/article/1658252-have-emerging-markets-gotten-oversold

When an index of an emerging market is up by 10% and the currency exchange rate to USD is down by 20%, then it is not profitable for us.

6   Intangibles

I give a score for each stock I evaluate. Occasionally some stocks with poor scores have great returns and vice versa. In general, the scoring system works. It has been proven statistically and repeatedly from my limited data. I stick with high-score stocks with some exceptions.

Once in a while I change my scoring system to adept to the current market conditions. To illustrate, the market bottom phase and early recovery phase of the market cycle favor value more than momentum/growth. Here are some of my recent experiences and strategies:

- I double or even triple my stake on stocks with high scores. In the longer term, they are consistently better winners than the average with some minor exceptions. Besides the score, look at the intangibles described in this article.

- Watch out for the stocks with outrageous metrics such as P/E of 4 or less. It could be a big lawsuit pending, an expiration of some important drugs, etc. Also, be careful with scores in the top 5%. From my statistics they do worse than the average. Their problems may not show up in the current financial statements.

- The technology of a tech company cannot be ignored even though the company's P/E is high, that I set a limit of 25 instead of 20 for other stocks. The value of the company's technology and patents will not be shown in the fundamental metrics except from the insiders' purchases at market prices.

  For example, IDCC rose about 40% in 2 days. There was a rumor that Google was buying the company and/or Apple was bidding on it too for its mobile technology. Charts usually would flag this kind of event. For non-charters, use the SMA-20% from Finviz.com. They could be a little late as the charts depend on rising prices.

- There are more acquisitions during a market bottom (same as early recovery). The companies with good technologies are bargains and the larger companies especially those in the same sector understand their values better than most of us. These potentially profitable companies will not be shown by their scores explicitly. When corporations have a lot of cash or the credit is cheap, they are looking for smaller companies to acquire or invest in. The candidates are usually small, beaten up, low-priced and having valuable intangible assets such as technologies, customer base and/or market share of the industry segment. 2009-2012 was just the perfect environment and the before that was 2003. I had at least one stock in each of these periods and they appreciated a lot.

- The opposite is Netflix, Chipotle in 1/2012 and Amazon in 1/2013. They are over-priced by any measure. However, the mentioned companies are investing in the future. The shorters (not for beginners) are having a tough time in making money on them. When their P/Es are higher than 40, watch out. Some could be OK in the mentioned companies, but usually they are not. Do not follow the herd and your due diligence will verify whether they will still go up.

  Use reward/risk ratio. It is based on experiences. To illustrate, if the company has the equal chance to go up 50% and go down 25%, then it is a buy and the reverse is a sell.

- The retail investor just cannot possibly know about some events until they actually happen. For example, ATSC dropped 15% due to losing its second primary customer. Fundamentals cannot predict this kind of events. Charts can signal this event, but usually they are too late unless you watch the chart all day long.

- After a quick run up, TZOO plunged due to missing some negligible earning expectations. It seems the original climbing prices already had the perfect earnings growth built-in.

  I do not understand why a company loses 10% of its market cap when it missed by 1% of the expected earnings. It could be driven up and down by the institutional investors. Evaluate the stock before you act. Acting opposite to the institutional investors could be very profitable for the right stocks. Avoid trading before the earnings announcement dates (about 4 times a year for most stocks).

- The following are not easily found in financial statements: industry outlook, patents, good will, market share, competition, product margins, management quality, lawsuits pending, potential acquisition, pension obligations, advertising icons, etc. That is why we need to read articles on the stocks in our buy list or our purchased stocks.

- The financial data could be fraudulent or manipulated. I do not trust small companies in emerging markets. I have been burned too many times. Check the company names such as foreign names, ADR and their headquarter addresses (from the company profile in most investing sites).

    Earnings can be manipulated with many accounting tricks. A jump in earnings from last year may not be as rosy as it looks. Check the footnotes in the accounting statements. I usually skip financial statements unless I have big purchases in mind as my time in investing is limited.

- Cash flow cannot be easily manipulated. It is good information whether the company will survive or not, but to me it does not prove to be a consistent predictor in my tests, but an important red flag for companies on their way to bankruptcy. Examples abound.

- Repeated one-time, non-recurring and extraordinary charges are red flags.

- Stay away from the companies where the CEOs are over-compensated. As of 7- 2013, Activision's CEO raised his salary by more than 600%, while the stock lost its value in double digits.

- Value stocks. Need to know why they become value stocks (i.e. fewer investors want to own) even they are financially sound. For example, there are two primary reasons for the downfall of a supplier to Apple: 1. Apple is declining in sales and 2. Apple is switching suppliers to replace their product. Technology companies are continually building better mouse traps. They could turn around in a year or so with better products.

Conclusion

Buying a stock is an educated guess that its stock price will rise. Fundamentals do not always work, but they work most of the time:

1. When we buy a value stock, we're swimming against the tide. Hence, we need to wait longer (usually more than 6 months) for the market to realize its value. The exception is the Early Recovery phase (see the

Market Cycle chapter) and it has faster and larger returns than most other stocks from most other stages of the market cycle.

2. Some metrics are misleading. Book value could be misleading for an established company such as IBM. The image of the cowboy in a tobacco company could be a very important asset that is not included in its financial statement.

3. The market is not always rational.

Afterthoughts

- Brand names of big companies are one of the most important intangibles. Here is a strategy to buy big companies in a down market. It has been proven that it works. However, do not just buy these companies without analysis.
http://seekingalpha.com/article/1324041-buying-brand-names-in-a-bear-market-can-make-you-rich

- The reputation of a company takes a long time to build but a bad incidence to destroy in the case of GM such as the delay in recalling the killer switches.

#Filler: Carrie Fisher, another sad American story

Unless drug addiction is part of the culture now as evidenced from the legalization of certain drugs, we're in a permissive society! Brits pushed opium as a nation when they had nothing better to trade. Opium killed millions of Chinese and bankrupted China. When we do not learn from history, we will repeat history. It is another sad story of fame and money and then losing it all. I bet she would be happier in a normal life instead of being born in a privileged class. Same can be said for many celebrities such as Presley, Houston and her daughter. RIP.

7 Qualitative analysis

This is the last analysis to evaluate a stock fundamentally. Then the next is technical analysis which is used to find an entry point (also the exit point) for the stock.

Where quantitative analysis fails and why

I find that some stocks with high scores fail and some stocks with low scores succeed as indicated by my performance monitor. The scoring system still works statistically for the majority of my stocks.

- Reasons why stocks with low scores perform in addition to the described in the last discussion:

    o Over-sold. The institutional investors (fund managers and pension managers) dump them first, and then followed by the retail investors. These big boys will buy these stocks back when they reach a certain price range. RSI(14), a technical indicator described in the Technical Analysis article, is useful to detect these over-sold stocks. This metric is readily available from many sites including Finviz.

    o The falling price (P) improves all fundamental metrics that have the stock price such as P/E and P/Sales. However, the trend of the price is down.

    o The company has turned around after fixing its problems and/or the market has changed for the better.

    o The current problems have been resolved but not known to the public. It includes resolving a lawsuit, a new product, a new drug, or a new big order, etc.

    o Heavy purchases by insiders. The company's outlook is not shown in its financial statements. Sometimes the insiders hide them so they can buy more of their companies' stocks for themselves.

- Reasons why stocks with high scores plunge in addition to the described in the previous discussion:

- The company's fundamentals and its prices have reached or closed to the maximum heights. They have no way to go but down. It is particularly true when the stock's timing rating is at or close to the highest point. TTWO that I gifted to my grandchildren had been 5-baggers in the last few years before it plunged in 2018.

- It has reached its potential value (or a target price) and it is time for many investors to take profits.

- Sector (or stock) rotation, particularly by institutional investors who drive the market.

- The outlook of the company, its sector and/or the market is deteriorating.

- The stock price may be manipulated. There are many reasons to pump and dump the stock. Shorting is not recommended for most investors. However, some experienced shorters make money consistently when they find valid reasons to short stocks.

- It could be due to a new serious lawsuit, a new competing product or drug, canceling a major order, etc.

- Downgrade by analysts. They could spot some bad events such as product defects, violations of regulations or accounting errors / frauds. The downgrades are more important than the upgrades that could have conflict of interest.

- The financial statement had been manipulated. The SEC may ask for an investigation.

- Does not meet the consensus in earnings announcements, which have been over-acted by many investors.

Qualitative Analysis

We need to do further analysis after the quantitative analysis and the intangible analysis. Check out the company's prospects. Check out the date of the article and any potential hidden agenda items from the author. Older articles may not have much value.

Be careful on 'pump-and-dump' manipulation written by authors with a hidden agenda. It has happened especially on small companies before even SeekingAlpha.com has its share. Here was an article that tells you to sell NHTC. There was another article to tell you to buy ARTX. They fit into this category.

The sources are:

1. Seeking Alpha.
   Type the symbol of the company to read as many articles on the company as you have time for. Today this site and many other similar sites require you to be a paid member. If you cannot find too many good articles, check out the articles from Finviz.com.

   Recently, I read an article on AMD and it said it may have good profits in the next two years with the game consoles. The outlook of a company is not shown by any fundamental metric which are far from favorable.

   Following a well-known writer, I bought IBM without doing my due diligence (my fault). It went down more than 15% quickly. You can learn from my mistakes.

2. Research reports from your broker. If you do not find many, open an account with one that provides such reports. Some subscription services such as Value Line provide such reports.

3. Yahoo!Finance board. Most comments are garbage. However, once in a while you find some great insights. Usually you cannot find any info from other sources on tiny companies.

4. The most recent company's financial statements. They are usually available in the company's web site.

5. 10-Ks from Edgar database (www.sec.gov/edgar). Check out new products and its potential competition, key customers, order backlog, research and development and pending lawsuits.

6. Check out the outlook of the sector the company is in and the company itself.

7. Check out its competitors.

8. Some companies are run by stupid people. I received information via my email saying that my mutual fund account could be treated as an abandoned property. I have been cashing dividend checks every year and why it would be considered as an abandoned property. I called them right away to close my account.

   The tall and handsome guy presented articulately how he would turn around JC Penny on TV. I could tell you right away that all his tricks had been tried by other companies such as Sears, and most did not work. The intelligent investor does not care about how handsome, how articulated, how rich his family is and how many advanced degrees from prestigious colleges he possesses. If he does not make sense, do not buy his preaching and his company's stock. [Update. As of 5/2020, J.C. Penny filed for bankruptcy protection. If you had this stock and my book, you would have saved a lot of money minus $10 for my book!]

9. Check out its business model. Some business models do not make business sense and some do. Here are some samples.

- Giving razors makes sense, as the customers have to buy the blades eventually and keep on buying blades for life.

- Supermarket M lowers prices on common merchandises such as Coke and it works. They make money by providing inferior (but profitable to them) products that you cannot compare prices easily such as meat and seafood.

  Eventually there will be a supermarket in my area to satisfy me both in price and quality or at least make a good tradeoff.
- Last week it had been brutally hot. I went to a Barns & Noble's bookstore to enjoy reading the updated books and enjoyed the air conditioning. When there are more free loaders like me than customers, this business model does not work.
- Market dumping works to capture the market. Microsoft used to do it with their new Office and Mail products that could not compete with the established products at the time. Google is following the same model to dump its equivalent products to compete with Office. Now, Microsoft is taking a dose of the same medicine.

8   Technical analysis (TA)

The basics

Technical analysis (a.k.a. charting) is easier to learn than you might expect. It represents the trend of the market (a stock or a group of stocks) graphically. If more investors are in the market, the market would move upwards until it changes direction. We divide the trends into short-term, intermediate-term and long-term.

The chartists usually do not consider fundamentals as they believe they have already been priced into the stock price and some fundamentals are not available to the public. To illustrate, a new drug has been discovered, the stock price of the company jumps initially by insiders purchases and the informed. Its fundamental metrics do not demonstrate this right away, but many investors are buying to boost up the stock price as evidenced by the technical indicators such as SMA for 20 or 50 days.

The volume is a confirmation. When the stock moves up or down by 10% with a low volume, the trend is not yet confirmed.

The trend of the stock price is not a straight line in most cases. Hence a trend line is usually drawn to indicate the direction of the stock. Many investors believe the stocks fluctuate in certain ranges (i.e. channels) and the chart draws the upper value (the resistance line) and the lower value (the support line). In theory, the price of a stock fluctuates within the resistance line (ceiling for understanding) and support (floor). When it reaches its support, it becomes a buy and vice versa for a sell. Most charts including Finviz.com would display these lines.

When the price passes out of the channel, it is called a breakout. Darvas, one of the oldest and most successful chartists, profited from the breakouts of the resistance line and believed the stock was close to the support line of the new channel. Hence it would be a long way up in theory.

If it were so simple, there will be no poor folks

It works most of the time, but do not place all your money on it. For chartists, 51% is great (the same for playing Black Jack). Some trends reverse very fast such as the bio drug stocks in 2015. You need to hedge your bets such as placing stop orders. Most do not want to spend their lives in watching the trend from a big screen.

Most novices use too many technical indicators and lose in their performances to the professionals. Recently, most chartists were not doing all that great and I did not find many books on their success than a decade ago. It could be due to too many followers in similar setups. I verified it with my recent testing using Finviz.com.

Simple Moving Average

The basic technical indicator is SMA-N. It is the average of the last N trade sessions. When N is 20 (or SMA-20), we classify it as short-term. Similarly, SMA-50 is an intermediate-term and SMA-200 is long-term. I prefer 50, 100 and 250. This trend duration is important. For example, do not want to place long-term purchases using the short-term SMA-50. There are many modifications to SMA such as giving more weight to recent data, but I have not found them any better. Finviz.com includes this information without charting (SMA-20, SMA-50 and SMA-100 in percentages).

Defining the trend periods is rather arbitrary. I use SMA-350 to detect the market plunges and SMA-100 for stocks. Weighted Moving Average weighs more weight on recent price data.

It can be used to determine whether we are in bull, bear or a sideways market using SMA-50 (or SMA-200 for longer term) for the market (using SPY), the sector (using an ETF for the sector and the specific stock. The trend is up when it the price is above the SMA and the reversal of the trend.

https://www.youtube.com/watch?v=jdYNaE5GJ0k&list=WL&index=5&t=609s

The trend is your best friend
Most traders use TA for trending in a short duration. Investors can also use TA to time the entry and exit points for better potential profits. Value investors usually are patient and they do bottom fishing and they search for 'oversold' condition using RSI(14). Again high volume is a confirmation.

Many sites provide charting free of charge such as Yahoo!Finance. Finviz.com provides a lot of technical indicators without charting such as SMA% and RSI(14). It also provides screen searching for stocks that meet your technical analysis criteria.

Hands on
Bring up Finviz.com and enter any stock symbol such as AAPL. You can see the daily prices of AAPL from about nine months ago to today. Three SMAs (Simple Moving Average) are displayed as SMA-20, SMA-50 and SMA-200. The first two are for short-term trends. When the price is above the SMA, it is expected to be trending up. Again, the trade volume is used as a confirmation.

You can also see the resistance line and the support line drawn. In theory, the stock will trade within these lines. When it exceeds its resistance line, it is called a breakout, and vice versa for a breakdown. Sometimes it displays some technical patterns such as Cup and Shoulder and Double Down (both are positive patterns).

Select Weekly data. The Candle chart is better described than the Daily chart. Candles give us better descriptions of the price: open, close, high and low. The green color indicates the price is up for the period (a week in this example) and the red color indicates a down period.

In addition, Finviz.com includes some technical indicators in the metric section such as RSI. Most other chart sites are similar in the basics. Use Finviz's Help and select Technical Analysis for more description. Investopedia has enhanced descriptions on this topic.

TA patterns

There are many TA patterns such as Bollinger Bands and MACD. The patterns are based on the stock prices and many times they prove to be correct predictions especially on stocks with high volume and high market caps. Patterns have been repeating themselves many times as they are driven by investors.

Sites for TA
There are many free sites for charts with explanations of their technical indicators. Popular ones include BigCharts.com, SmallCharts.com and Yahoo!Finance. Fidelity includes some unique features in its charts such as P/E.

Why I do not use TA as a primary tool for stock picking

My investing style is different from a day trader's. I prefer to 'Buy Low and Sell High' instead of 'Buy High and Sell Higher'. I try to find the real bottom price. TA will not find the bottom very easily but it tracks the trend better. As a bargain hunter, I do not expect the stock will rise fast as I'm usually swimming against the tide. However, value stocks could stay in the low price for a long time (i.e. value trap). I like to select stocks that turn around as evidenced by the SMA-20 and SMA-50.

With that said, my momentum portfolio has appreciated consistently and usually has the best performing stocks among all my portfolios. It is based on the timely grade from my subscriptions plus the metrics on timing.

Most chartists would also tell you to buy the stocks that have broken out (i.e. higher than the resistance line) and/or stocks at their highs. Contrary to value investing, you should exit when the trend reverses. The reversal could happen very fast and hence protect your portfolio by setting up stop loss (preferably with trailing stop) orders.

My opinion

I do not want to argue whether TA is good for you or not. You need to find that out. Most likely, the day traders and very short-term traders will profit more from TA than the investors seeking value stocks for the long-term gains.

Random remarks

Even if you do not use technical analysis, you should spend some time in learning it. It is better to marry fundamentals and TA. My random remarks are:

- The Institutional investors (insurance companies, pension funds, mutual funds, etc.) use TA and they MOVE the market. A lot of times it becomes a self-fulfilling prophecy. It is better to join them as most of us cannot beat them.

- Day traders take advantage of the institutional investors by spotting their trends.

- Most TA stocks should be good sized and have large average daily volumes. I prefer to use TA on value stocks to prevent long-term losses.

- I do know some folks making big money using TA, but I know more making good money using fundamentals. Since TA predicts the market better in the shorter term, its practitioners may have to pay higher taxes (in today's tax laws) in taxable accounts.

- Our objective should be making money with the least risk. Once you claim to belong to a certain group of either Fundamental or TA, you will be biased and forget your primary objective in investing.

- TA tracks the last two big market plunges (2000 and 2007) pretty well. The chart will not warn you right away for the upcoming plunge (as it depends on past data) to avoid the initial losses, but they will warn you to avoid bigger losses.

Afterthoughts

- Besides searching for stocks that have potential breakouts, we should check the stocks we owned for potential breakdowns.
  Technical Analysis tutorial.
  https://www.YouTube.com/watch?v=GENBVwV8PMs

  SMA tutorial.
  https://www.YouTube.com/watch?v=Na-ctpPsnks

Links

Fidelity video: Technical Analysis
https://www.fidelity.com/learning-center/technical-analysis/chart-types-video

9 Tom's conservative strategy

Tom's conservative strategy

The following is a summary of Tom's conservative strategy as described in his profile in Seeking Alpha web site. Use it as an example and modify it to fit your investing philosophy. You need to ignore your friends telling you how much money he is making when the market is up. You also need not to tell them how much money you're not losing otherwise you do not have any friend.

I believe the best performance is achieved matching a strategy to the current market conditions and there is no Holy Grail in investing.

Click here for Tom's strategy.
(http://tonyp4idea.blogspot.com/2012/05/tom-armisteads-investment-strategy.html)

A winning strategy for couch potatoes

My friend Tom (no relationship) has a very similar strategy similar to Tom's. My friend is making money with the least risk. He only buys stocks after the market crashes and sell stocks when the market rises. Ignore all market pundits. It is recommended to anyone who does not have time to monitor his/her investment.

Enhance a good strategy.
Following the favorable stages to trade in the market cycle described in this book, buy in the Early Recovery phase (about 1 ½ year after the crash or use the entry point described in the chapters on Market Timing), sell in one or two years after and maintain cash for the rest of the time.

Optionally add a small amount of purchases in Nov. 1 and sell them in April 1. Optionally buy in Dec. 1 and sell in Feb. 1 to take advantage of the best (statistically) period of the year. Add long term bonds when the interest rate is high (say more than 5%) and you do not have to sell these bonds.

Spend the rest of the time in the comfortable couch (i.e. enjoying life) or sip some fancy tropical drink served by some beautiful tropical lady in some nice tropical island. Not a bad strategy!

Top down approach

1. Is it a good time to buy stocks (via market timing)?
2. What sectors to buy?
3. Screen out about 10 stocks in that sector.
4. Further evaluate each stock.
5. Optionally, use Technical Analysis to see the best time and price to buy the selected stocks.
6. Periodically monitor your stocks. Sell some if necessary and go to Step 1.

When you buy at the bottom, buy value stocks only.

The easiest retirement planning system

Have a budget and live within your means. Buy good stuffs that last for a long time. After saving enough cash for emergency and planned expenses such as vacation, new car, college, etc., invest your extra money in a retirement account (Roth IRA if allowable) with 80% in a market ETF and 20% in a short-term bond ETF.

Run the chart described in the market cycle chapters once a month. If the chart tells you to exit the market, move all to cash. Reenter the market when the chart tells you so. It beats most if not all of your financial plans from the best experts money can buy.

Afterthoughts

- My late friend had a 'buy and hold strategy' that worked pretty well. Most of his stocks were big companies. He died with a house worth more than a million and many millions in stocks. His only mistake was not to transfer more of his stocks to his heirs before his death. He died on the year when the estate exemption returned back to a million. Uncle Sam was the biggest winner and won big without any effort.

10   A turnaround strategy on value stocks

Many value stocks tend to stay in this phase for a long time. When the turnaround starts, it could be very profitable.

Market Timing

Do not buy any stock when the market is risky as described elsewhere in the book. Actually you should sell most of the stocks when the market is risky.

Buy Metrics

Metric	Value	Conservative	Aggressive
General			
Market Cap	>300 M	>1,000 M	>100 M
Price	> 2	>10	>1
Avg. Volume	>20,000	>50,000	>10,000
USA	Only	Only	Foreign but listed in USA
Fundamental			
Forward P/E	<15	<10	<25
Earning Gr Q-Q	>5%	>8%	>3%
ROE	>10	>15	>5
P / FCF	<10	<8	<15
Debt / Equity	<.5	<.25	<1
Technical			
SMA-50%	>10	>15	>5
Misc.			
Blue Chip	A or B	A	A or B
Growth			
Fidelity	>6	>8	>5
IBD	>60	>90	>50
Vector Vest	>=1	>=0.8	>=12
Value Line	>5%	>10%	>5%
Proj. 3-5% return			
Zacks	>=4	5	>=4
ASSS	>=2	>=5	>=2

The assignment values for the metrics are not fixed; feel free to change it according to your own risk level. I do have suggestions for conservative investors and aggressive investors.

Some of the metrics are not readily available in Finviz.com and the following describes how to modify them.

Explanation

- Market Cap. The free version of Finviz.com does not allow you to specify the range. Use 'Any' and then select the stocks according to the specified values. Average Volume has the similar restriction.
- The conservative values for Market Cap, Price and Average Volume try to select larger companies. The aggressive values try to select smaller companies, which historically are more risky but perform better.
- I prefer 'USA' for Country. Stay away from small companies from developing countries unless you can trust their financial statements.
- Forward P/E measures the value of the stock. Ensure "E" (Earnings) is positive. I prefer it over P/E (from the last twelve months).
- Earnings Growth Quarter to last Quarter is preferred to be positive unless it is during a recession.
- ROE measures how well the company has been managed.
- P/FCF. "Price / Free Cash Flow" cannot be manipulated easily. Together with low "Debt / Equity", it measures whether the company would bankrupt.
- SMA-50%. Some stocks tend to stay in a value stage for a long while (termed value trap). We like to select stocks just starting being noticed and on its way up.
- Misc. Many sites have evaluated the stocks for us. Some only let their customers to access such information, some are available for free trials or are available from the library.
- ASSS is my scoring system.

With the above, I have 35 stocks on 10/28/16. If you need 10 stocks for further evaluation, try to sort Forward P/E in descending order and select the top 10. If you cannot find any or substantially less than normal, it implies the market is risky, so take a break. If the performances of the last few stocks you selected are poor, take a break too as the market conditions do not favor the value metrics we specified.

Qualitative analysis

Double click on the stock and read as many articles described on the stock as possible. If it meets all the criteria, buy the stock. Recommend to use market orders for large companies in a non-volatile market (when the average daily fluctuation is less than 0.5%). If the selected stock is the one you just sold, make you only buy it after 31 days to avoid Wash Sale penalty.

Keeping informed

Check the company updates of the stock you owned every month. One easy way is to enter the stocks in a portfolio in SeekingAlpha.com.

Sell the stock

Re-evaluate the stocks every 6 months.

If it does not meet the criteria or the market is risky, sell it. If it is only a few days away from the long-term capital gain, sell the losers right away or hold on the winner for a few more days.

Re-balance the portfolio after a stock has been sold. Ensure it is diversified enough into large/small cap and sectors.

Top-down Investing

It is similar to the above. Find the sectors that perform the best last month. Under Finviz.com, select the best sector under 'sector' one at a time. Several sites such as Fidelity compare the stock to the averages of stocks in the same sector.

11   The best strategy

Note. Most parameters described here such as SMA-20% and Short% can be found from Finviz.com

It is Buy Low and Sell High.

It is simple but most retail investors just do the opposite: Buy High and Sell Low. The flow of money to/from money market funds turns out to be a reliable contrary indicator.

The Early Recovery in 2003 and 2009 and the later part of June, 2012 could be the best time to buy.

The above represents buy at low prices and sell at high prices. Considering P/E (positive 'E' only), buy at low P/E of a stock, a sector and the market (via an ETF) and sell them respectively at high P/E.

Here are some hints when to buy and sell with this strategy:

- Sell when everyone including your silly mother-in-law is making good money and all participants think they're financial geniuses. It could be the riskiest time. The high interest rate (my yardstick is over 5% for Fed Discount rate, the best rate the Fed lends to the banks) usually confirms this as folks falsely expect better return even they pay more on interest to borrow money to buy stocks.

- Do not buy the stocks that were the bubble-forming stocks such as the technology stocks in 2001-2002 and the bank stocks in 2008-2009 as some 'optimists' think it is time to return and usually they're wrong.

    Do not think the stock is a good deal when it loses half of its value. Buy them only when the root problem has been fixed. The best time to return to the market after a market plunge is usually two years after the market plunge (2003 for the market plunge in 2000 and 2009 for the market plunge in 2007/2008). Many bubble stocks never recover and many of these stocks take more than 3 years to recover. Their prices appear to be low, but no one can predict the bottom unless it goes to zero.

- Be careful on the sector or group of stocks that have winning streak for more than two years. Most likely they will correct. Use stop loss to protect your profits if you want to keep them.

  You could have saved a lot if you use this strategy on tech stocks in 2000. As of 2015, dividend stocks could be the next sector to burst but only time can tell. Do not fall in love with a stock. Yesterday's winners could be tomorrow's losers, and vice versa.

  'Buy and hold' is dead since 2000. We have two market plunges with an average loss of about 45% from their peaks.

- Do not buy dividend stocks solely for their dividends. Most of them are matured companies; most have less growth and hence less appreciation potential. They usually lose less value in a recession after dividends. Income investors are chasing them for higher dividends than bonds.

  Except from Roth accounts, when you withdraw from your retirement accounts, your dividends will be treated as income. Check the current tax rates for income and dividend from taxable accounts.

- Buy value stocks that seem to be bottomed. It is hard to identify the bottom. When the appreciation potential outweighs the risk, it could be a buy.

- No one can predict consistently the market bottom. However, use your better judgment with educated guesses to gain an edge. Refer to the exit point using the 350-day SMA from the chapter on detecting market plunges.

- Buy the stocks that have been losing money but their burn rates can last for the entire recession. They're risky but the potential profits are great. There were many in 2003 and 2009. Even in a bad economy in 2012, a few corporations had historically low P/Es.

- Buy value stocks with a turnaround sign such as when the SMA-50% is positive.

- Buy against the experts who have unconvincing predictions. They usually exaggerate the rosy outlooks of the companies in order to sell the stocks they own. This is one of the few times you should bet against them. Use your better judgment to ensure how false their predication would be.

Using Citicorp (symbol C) as an example

Following the chapter on avoiding bank stocks, buying this stock at $550 a share could be avoided. After the big plunge in 2008, I believe it has long-term profit potential. Accumulate this stock if you believe C will be profitable in 10 years (2024) or so. Do not sell it unless there is potential for a market plunge. If so, buy it back after the plunge. One's opinion.

With our market timing (defending sector may return in two years), I checked it in mid 2009, about 2 years after the start of the market plunge. Optionally I could use the SMA-350 of the stock to determine the reentry point. However, it had no meaning due to the big plunge from $550. On 8/2009, C's P/E was negative, so I did not buy it.

Alternatively buy it for every big drop in P/E regardless of the current price as follows. We started when the P/E is about 40. Normally I buy it when the P/E is at around 20. Take an exception for turnaround stocks.
The above is for illustration only, so the numbers are not precise.

As of 6/12/2014, I expected a correction, so I sold it at about $48. I only trade this kind of stocks when I see long-term appreciation potential. The other three important metrics are P/B, P/S and RSI(14). Use forward (expected) P/E if possible. The most important metric for lenders is the quality of the loans, which is hard to evaluate for retail investors. The other factor is any serious, pending lawsuits. When Lehman Brothers was gone, the governments will chase after the institutions that sold the derivatives.

The second best strategy

Buy high and sell higher.

When everyone is looking for stocks with the highest value, there may not be any such stocks available. It seems to contradict with my best strategy but it is not. Fundamentals may not show everything about the company such as a new drug, a new product... The all-time high prices usually show that. Buy the stock when it is over the 50-day simple moving average (50 or 200 days depending on how long you usually hold a stock) via Finviz.com.

Buying fully-priced stocks is dangerous even it may be profitable. To protect your profits:

- Be extra careful in risky market; I prefer not to buy any stock when the market is risky.

- Set stop loss orders. Recommend 10% (or 15% for volatile stocks) less than the current price. If you set 5% stop, it would be stopped out for normal fluctuations.

- Use Technical Analysis. When the price drops below the moving average you used, sell it. When RSI (14) is high (over 70), check out the reason as it could be overbought.

If you are not very sure, sell half of it. You will not get broke for taking profits.

As in life, there are no guarantees, but using a proven technique / discipline is far better than trading without one. Paper trading to ensure the strategy fits the current market conditions, your personal tolerance and requirements.

The third strategy

Buy very high and sell even higher.

It is the riskiest. These stocks could be bubble stocks moved by institution investors and then moved even higher by retail investors. It may take a while before the institution investors rotate to another sectors / stocks and/or take profit.

My strategy is to follow the herd but ensure you're ready to exit.

- Find them. Usually they have break-outs. They pass the resistance, a technical term. Now, they are in the low of the support line, so they have a long way to go to the next resistance line. It has to be confirmed with its daily volume such as 3 times or more than the average daily volume. Usually they are in the 52-week highs.

- Usually they are large caps with high trade volumes. My range is 100M to 5B. Be careful on stocks ranging from 100M to 500M. They may appreciate a lot on the positive side; they are risky and they can be manipulated easier. Stocks from 1B to 5B appreciation potential is lesser than 100M to 500M.

- Do not short them.

- Buy them ignoring the fundamentals as they are moved up with the herd sometimes for a reason and sometimes not. Alternatively, use options.

- Set mental stop losses. Adjust the stops periodically after they have appreciated.

- Watch them every day. Bring up Finviz.com and enter the sector ETF the stock belongs to and the stocks. Pay attention to SMA200%: The higher it is, the higher chance it is peaking. When RSI(14) is over 70% (65% for sectors), most likely it is overbought. When SMA-20% is negative, there is a good chance of reversing the trend to downward.

Buy and monitor

I usually sell my stocks that have fulfilled my objectives or admitted I have made a mistake. However, some stocks keep on rising and I may miss many 3 or more baggers.

I gifted many appreciated stocks to my family members. My grandchildren will keep them for a long while. Here are the stocks I gave on 5/1/2015 (the date I gifted) and the performances today (5/12/2018).

Stock	Total Return	Annualized return
CSCO	58%	19%
STX	88%	29%
TTWO	377%	124%
Average	174%	57%
Compare to:		
SPY	29%	10%

My point is "buy and hold" is still valid for many stocks. Buy low when they have been temporarily ignored. These stocks should have long-term potentials as they will be held for a long while. My actual performance is substantially more as I bet at least double more in TTWO.

Instead of "Buy and Hold", you need buy and monitor. When they have serious problems such as Circuit City, Radio Shack, Sears…, do not hesitate to sell them.

When you time the market, ensure buy back these stocks you sold during the recovery phase of the market cycle.
My long-term grade

They compose of the following (using metrics from Finviz.com): low Forward P/E, low Debt/Eq, Cash/sh, larger Market Cap, ROE, low RSI(14), Insider Own, Sales Q/Q, EPS Q/Q, SMA200… In addition, they have good products for the future and invest heavily in research.

Filler: Happy Mother's Day Poem
(This is my translation from an unknown Chinese author)

I cried at two unforgettable times in my life.

The first time when I came to this world.
The second time when you left this world.

The first time I did not know but from your mouth.
The second time you did not know but from my heart.

Between these two crises, we had endless laughs.
But for the last 30 years, we had joyful laughs that had been repeated, repeated…

You treasured every laugh.
I remember every laugh for the rest of my life.

12   Order prices

Market orders
It is simply trading the stock at the prevailing market price. Place market orders only when it is necessary as stocks price can easily be manipulated especially on stocks with low trading volumes. To avoid manipulations, do not place market orders after hours.

However, in a rising market, many fast rising stocks can only be bought via market orders. Many winners never take a breather on their way up. In this case, you can only buy the stock via market orders.

Consider bid and ask. A 'bid' is the price a potential buyer would like to buy while the 'ask' is a potential seller would like to sell. Your market price is usually the worst price in either case, but it is a guarantee that you would trade the stock. A large spread would mean that it would take a longer time to use a limit order and/or the trade volume of the stock is small.

In my momentum portfolio on 11/2013, I placed a sell price for GERN far higher than the market price. Surprisingly I sold it for this price making an annualized return of 1,176% for holding it for 21 days. When there are few or no other sellers for the stock, the market price would be the price you set. If I cannot sell it in the next 9 days (30 days is my holding period for momentum stocks), I would set it lower. Update: One year later, GERN lost 29%.

Sensible discounts
I prefer to buy the stock at the price closest to the last trade price (to most it is the market price) via a limit order. I seldom lose buying these orders. Sometimes I use the day's lowest price to buy (or the highest to sell) plus a penny (or minus a penny for sell prices to sell).

My other purchase strategy is using 0.15% or 0.25% less than the current prices for stocks I really want. For some promising stocks, I buy them at almost the market price and then place another order on the same stock at 0.5% less than the last traded price (and sometimes 2% depending on the current market trend).

We all want to buy less and sell at higher prices. However, if the trade price is too far away from the current market price (such as 5% from the market price), these trades may never be executed. I have had a long list of buy orders that were not executed and turned out to be big gainers. Learn from my bad experiences.

Use a good discount (such as 10% from the market price) if you believe the market, the sector or the stock will dip by 10%. After you bought the stock, you place a sell order 10% more than the price you paid for it hoping the stock will return to the original price and you pocket 10%. Wishful thinking! However, it has happened to me several times primarily due to temporary market dips.

It works when there is a correction and/or the stock is very volatile. It is usually within the 5% range to take advantage of these situations, not the 10% as described. For a 10% plunge, it usually is due to some serious problem of the company surfacing. One common reason is not meeting its earnings expectation and in this case it usually continues its downward trend.

Larger discounts on a falling market
During a falling market (or a mild correction), 3% less than the current prices for buy orders may be fine for some stocks (use 5% for volatile stocks). To illustrate, I placed about 10 of these orders over the last two months during a market dip. Most of the orders were filled. When the market is plunging, do not buy any stock.

Caterpillar and Cisco were some of my buys at these discounts. They were in my watch list to buy. Initially these shares often fall even lower as the trend was downward. As of 12/18/12, CAT earned me from 3% and 14% (bought in 6/12 and 7/12) and CSCO bought in 7/14/12 returned about 34%. My original objective: Buy deeply-valued stocks, wait and sell them when the economy returns.

When you predict the market will dip by 5%, set your buy orders accordingly. Again, predictions are just educated guesses. From my experience, they work most of the time but not all of the time.

On the day of the earnings announcement, the fluctuation of the stock is usually high. Check any change in the earnings estimate before the announcement and act accordingly. Zacks is supposed to be a useful tool to predict earnings estimates. Do not leave orders during the earnings announcement dates, which can be found in Finviz. When the earning turns out to be good, the stock price surges and your order will not be executed.

When the earnings are bad, the stock price will plunge usually and you most likely over-payed.

Option expiration dates usually cause more volatility. Retail investors do not have to be concerned except you may use wider stops. In theory, dividend days have little effect on the stock price as it will be lowered by the dividend amount.

High volume of a stock could mean opportunity

High volume usually increases the stock price volatility. If the volatility of a stock increases substantially (such as doubling its average daily volume), there could be important news on the company, recommendation changes from a major analyst or trading by the institutional investors. It usually takes the institutional investors a week to trade a stock with their sizable positions.

Many times it is started by the insiders who know about the breaking news of a stock before it is publicized. Some investment services / sites specialize in identifying the increasing volumes on these stocks.

Because day traders do not want to leave any open positions overnight, higher volatility occurs at the end of the day. It is the same on the day (usually on Friday) when the options are expiring.

Monitor your trade prices
You cannot tell whether you are paying a fair price without keeping a record. To illustrate, you're paying 1% less than the market prices in buying stocks. You may have missed buying some winners. If the 1% you saved is smaller than the appreciation of the stocks you would have bought at market prices, then you should adjust the buy prices to 0.5% less than the market price and monitor again.

Market trend makes a difference too. When the market is trending up, buying any stock would most likely be profitable and usually the purchase orders with higher discounts will not be executed.

Follow the same logic on sell orders. Need to have at least 25 stock purchases (and potential purchases) to make the conclusion meaningful. If you do not trade a lot, you will not have enough data to verify. As described, I prefer not to place an order during the earnings announcement dates which can be found in Finviz.com. If you cannot buy the stock, consider to use market order the next day. With most brokers offer no commission trades, the "All or none" option is not valid.

Good prospects
When you find gems especially those stocks that are followed by analysts, buy them at market prices and consider doubling the bet if you are really sure you have a winner. From my super stock screens, I spotted NHTC. I placed several bets and one market order. All of them were NOT executed except with the market order. At the end of the day NHTC is up 18% and my executed order is up 14%. I did not have the best buy but made a good profit. NHTC was on its way to a huge appreciation and I sold it too early. I have earned not to sell a winner and protect the profit with a stop.

Lower the buy for risky stocks (if the beta from Finviz is greater than 1 for example) even if they have good fundamentals.

Quality over quantity
If your time is limited, spend all the time on researching one stock one at a time. However, you need to own at least 3 stocks (more stocks for a large portfolio) for your diversification purposes.

Double your normal purchase position on stocks that look great after the research. For risky stocks that look good, you may want to halve your normal purchase position to cut down on the risk. If you are less risk tolerant, do not buy risky stocks at all. My results are not conclusive on risky stocks but I do get a good sleep.

A recent example
Recently I sold EA with $1 more than my order price but $2 less than the current price of the day, which was the earnings announcement day. I do recommend not placing orders right before the earnings announcement day for the stock. If the earnings are good, you do not get all the profit as in this real example; my broker did get me $1 more. If the earnings are bad, you will not sell it any way. It is the same for buying stocks.

Afterthoughts
- Besides luck, the smart investor never sells at the peak but usually within 10% of the peak. No one can predict the peaks consistently.

- I made mistakes like most of you. One time my buy price was higher than the last price executed. Luckily my broker adjusted it to the right price but I may not be that lucky next time. Several times I switched the buy price and sell price by mistake. One time it was due to my boss coming by that forced me to enter my order hastily. Try to avoid the first hour of a trade session.
- Some experts do not suggest their clients to buy stocks on the way down. With respect, I offer opposing arguments.

    - It is fine to buy them on the way down, if you have the conviction that the company or the economy will recover.
    - No one knows where the bottom is, but averaging down could be beneficial if the company or the economy can recover. Check why its stock price is falling and whether the company can fix its problems. Some major problems are only temporary or easy to fix.
    - Most of my big profits are made by buying close to the bottom prices on stocks that have a good potential to recover.
    - Many value stocks are on sale when the market dips. The most favorable time is in the Early Recovery, a phase in the market cycle defined by me.
    - Most experts agree that: The best time to buy is when there is blood in the street. It is demonstrated by the year 2003 and 2009.
    - Contrarians never follow the herd, but you need to have a good reason to be contrary. I recommended Apple in 2013 when every institutional investor was dumping Apple.
    - Stocks are manipulated via selling shorts. When the shares of a stock to short (like over 30% of shorts) are running out, there is a good chance for a short squeeze. Ensure the company being shorted heavily is not heading into bankruptcy.
- Make good money when you are right only 45% of the time by: 1. Limit your losses via stops and 2. Place higher stakes on stocks with higher appreciation potential.
- Some make money on earnings announcement (found in Finviz.com). Earnings would amplify the stock price by at least 5%. Once in a while, there are exceptions. In the last quarter of 2015, Disney posted great results, but the stock dropped. It could be that the market even expected better results or the market is not rational. I believe the later in this case.

13   When to sell a stock

There are many reasons to sell a stock as follows.

Personal

1. Has met my targets/objectives.
    It could be a 10% gain in a very short-term swing, x% return in 4 months for a short-term swing or y% gain after a year for long-term trades. Define x and y depending on your risk tolerance and how often you trade.

    I bought 4 stocks in one day during the August, 2015 correction and placed sell orders with 10% more than my purchase prices. I sold one in a day and another one within a month. This is my strategy for correction – sometimes it works and sometimes it does not.

    Never look back. Do not blame yourself when the prices are better than your trade prices. When the market is volatile, use a higher percent of the current prices. Be disciplined. Stay on the same strategy and detach yourself from emotions.

2. Realize that we have made a mistake. Do not let your ego block your eyes. It could be due to bad analysis, bad, data, unexpected fraud, lawsuits, and/or unforeseeable events that you have no control of. It is better to get out with a small loss. I prefer a 25% loss as a threshold for long-term strategies and a 10% (or less for some strategies) loss for short-term strategies.

    We have to ensure whether it is a mistake or not. If the 'mistake' is just bad luck or due to conditions we cannot possibly predict or control, then it is not a mistake. If it is a mistake, learn from it. When we diversify, one bad loss should not cause a big dent in our portfolios. The stop loss is a good tool most of the time except when there is a flash crash.

    If the criteria have been faithfully followed and it does not work well, check out whether your criteria are wrong, or it does not work on the current market conditions.

3. When we have too many stocks in the same sector, we will want to replace some stocks to better diversify our portfolios.

   When the sector is rising, we want to weigh more on that sector at the expense of diversification, and vice versa. Set a limit of how many sectors you should hold.

4. Need cash for living expenses.

5. To reduce a tax burden by selling some losers. Tax consideration should not be the primary reason for selling. Take advantage of the favorable tax treatment for long-term capital gains. In short, sell losers within the short term limit (currently a year), and sell winners after 365 days; check the current tax laws.

   Harvest tax losses. Sell losers and buy back similar stocks (or same stock after 31 days to avoid wash sale). It is not too clear in which you can buy back the same loser in your children's account under the current tax law.

6. To take advantage of a lower tax. In 2013, we can pay virtually zero (except the increase of tax on social security payment) Federal income taxes on long-term capital gains when our income is below a specific tax bracket (15% as of 2015). Check out the current tax laws. Evaluate the sold winners for a possible buy back.

Market Timing

7. When the market or the sector plunges, sell stocks or stocks within the sector.

   For temporary peaks, evaluate which stocks in your portfolio to sell based on fundamentals. The objective is to raise cash for buying opportunities.

Deteriorating appreciation potential

8. There may be some stocks that have a better appreciation potential than the ones you currently own. Churning the portfolio by replacing better stocks may cost some brokerage commissions (some are free

today) and taxes for taxable accounts, but it improves the quality and the appreciation potential for the entire portfolio.

9. The company's fundamentals have changed for the worse. If you use a scoring system, compare the current score with the score you actually bought the stock for. Apple is a good example from 2013 to 2015. Buy when the fundamentals are good and sell when they are not.

   The basic fundamentals are expected P/E, the quarter-to-quarter earnings growth rate / the sales growth rate, and Debt /Equity.

   When your stocks have passed the peak and started to decline, sell them. When they are heading to bankruptcy, sell them fast.

Hints that the fundamentals are degrading

Evaluate the stocks you own at least every 6 months and check their daily news at least once a week that can be easily done using Seeking Alpha's portfolio function.

- The cash flow is decreasing fast. Cash flow is not a particularly good predicative indicator for appreciation, but a good indicator on whether the company will survive. This metric is very hard to manipulate.

- A new or pending lawsuit. Check out how serious the lawsuit is and be aware that a minor lawsuit can be ignored. Companies always sue against each other.

- A big drop in sales. Do not be alarmed when a new product, or a new drug is going to replace a major product. Compare sales to the same quarter of prior year to avoid seasonal fluctuations (Q-to-Q info I available from Finviz.com).

- Management deteriorates- One hint is the deteriorating ROE from the last quarter.

- The extravagant life style of the CEO and the many easy loans to officers.

- Poor operations. They include recalls of products such as the GM recall on ignition switches, product secrets being stolen and customers' credit card info being stolen. Boeing's 747-Max is a warning call.

- A successful product from the competitor, or the current product is losing its market share, or becoming a low-profit commodity.

- Insiders and/or institutional investors are dumping the companies' stocks far more than the averages (2% for me) especially in heavy volumes and by more than one insider.

    o Have more than one insider dumping a lot of the stock within a month and no insider purchase in that month.

    o Have more than one insider decrease their holdings by more than 10%.

- When the SEC or any government agency pays attention to a company, it usually means bad news.

- Deceptive accounting practices have been discovered.

- Increasing receivable and/or inventory at an alarming rate.

- Earnings have been restated too many times.

- Short percentage is increasing fast – someone found something wrong with the company.

- The invalidity of 'one-time charges'.

- Abnormal return rate of the company's pension fund comparing to the average of the companies in the same sector.

- Too many and too costly reconstructing charges.

- The entire stock market is plunging as indicated by our chart in detecting market crashes.

- The stock price does not move up with good news. It shows the price has peaked.

- The accumulation amount is far less than the sold amount. When the stock price is up, the accumulation is less than the sold stocks when the stock price was down the last time. It indicates that no more accumulation is ahead and hence the stock will be down most likely.

Afterthoughts

- Another article on this topic.
  http://buzz.money.cnn.com/2013/04/05/stocks-sell/
  An article from Investopedia. Nothing new but it is worth having the same second opinion.
  http://www.investopedia.com/financial-edge/0412/5-tips-on-when-to-sell-your-stock.aspx

- It also depends on your strategies. I sell most of my stocks in my momentum portfolio within a month. At least one strategy I know of does not keep any stock during the peak stage of the market cycle – the easiest time to make money but also the riskiest time.

  If you use charts for trading, sell the stocks that are below your moving averages or other technical analysis indicators. Personally I do not use charts for making sell decisions due to my limited time.

- Sell when the company is heading into bankruptcy as described before. The red flags are: 1. Negative cash flow. 2. Heavy insiders dumping the stocks. 3. Pending major lawsuit. 4. Fraud from the management.

- Risky periods for a stock.
  Earnings announcement (4 times a year), settling a major lawsuit and/or during a FDA event in approving a drug are risky periods for a stock. A fluctuation more than 5% in either direction is normal. Some use options to buy insurance. Most ignore it. For the majority of the time, heavy insider purchase is a good indicator. There are rumors (or educated guesses) on earnings before their announcements. Zacks is supposed to be a good subscription for earnings estimates.

Section IV: Bonus

Most free sites do not subdivide sectors into subsectors.

1   Market timing example

The market is making new highs. There are always two camps of market timers. One camp predicts a crash is coming while the other predicts it will continue making new highs. This article includes both arguments and suggests how and what actions you need to take to protect your investments.

Management summary

The market is fundamentally unsound evidenced by fundamental metrics but technically sound evidenced by technical metrics that both will be described in this article. The data were obtained on 09/22/2018. The market has not changed a lot as of 01/2020.

Suggested actions
No one predicts the market correctly and consistently. Otherwise there are no poor folks. Moving the risky investments such as most stocks to cash too early would miss the potential profits. Moving it too late would risk the loss of your stocks.

Your actions depend on your risk tolerance. If you are conservative such as a retiree, you may want to have a larger portion of your investments in lower risk such as CDs and bonds. You can take one of the following three actions or combine all of the three actions.

1. When the market turns to technically unsound, it is time to move your stocks to cash. The market timing indicators may give false signals. In this case, the indicator would tell you to move back to stocks. Most likely you do not lose much except dealing with the consequences of taxes in non-retirement accounts.
2. Move a portion of your risky investments into cash, laddered CDs and/or short-term bonds. Again, the size of the portion depends on your risk tolerance.
3. Use stops. The sell orders would be changed to market orders when the stocks dip below prices specified by you. I prefer to use SPY or other ETF to determine the market direction. Some sectors and some stocks

move faster than others. In one crash, my energy stocks were still profitable while the market was tanking. Eventually these energy stocks caught up and fell fast. Today's highly profitable stocks are FAANG stocks as a group.

I propose and prefer 'manual stop orders' to prevent market manipulation. However, usually large ETFs cannot be manipulated easily. Manipulators try to profit from your stop orders. Set a stop order price in your `mind. When the stock falls to that specified price, sell it via a market order.

My friend confirmed my "manual stop order":

"High-frequency trading via Algo Trading Strategy can see exactly where pre-set trailing stops are and sweep across them (play them) like strings on a violin. Pre-set a trailing stop and it is bound to be triggered because Algo hunt them down. Then watch the market rip higher."

Analysis: Fundamentals and Technical

It consists of Fundamental Analysis and Technical Analysis. The former measures how expensive the current market is and the latter measures the trend of the market.

Many metrics were obtained from Finviz.com as of 9/22/2018 while others are obtained from other websites. With the exception of Fidelity.com, all websites described here are free and readily available. It also serves as a guide on how you can do your own market timing especially after a few months.

The following chart uses SPY to represent the market of the top 500 stocks. It is market cap weighted. It means the higher the market cap the stock, the higher percent of the stock is represented in the index. It turns out most are riskier FAANG stocks.

Enter Finviz.com in your browser and enter SPY. I am not responsible for any errors.

Indicator	Pass	Current Value	Indicating
• Technical			
Death Cross[1]		SMA-50 = 2.3% & SMA-200 = 6.3%	Pass

Technical Analysis: 350 SMA%[2]	>0	Price above the SMA-350.	Pass
RSI(14)	<70	61	Pass
Duration (yr.)	<5	10	Fail
		Overall	**Pass**
• Fundamental Valuation			
P/E[3]	<15.7	25.4	High by 62%. Fail.
Shiller P/E[3]	<16.6	33.5	High by 102%. Fail.
P/B[3]	<2.78	3.52	High by 27%. Fail.
P/S[3]	<1.50	2.33	High by 55%. Fail.
Oil price	30-100	70.71	Pass
Interest rate[6] T-Bill 1 months[7]	<5	2.05	Pass
T-Bill 3 months[7]	Yield	2.18	
T-Bill 30 years[7]	Curve	3.20	Pass
Flow to Equity[4]		-3.371M	Fail
Flow to bond[4]		7.206M	
Corporate debt/GDP[8]	<40	45%	High by 13%. Fail.
USD[5]		Strong	Fail
Gold		High	Fail
Bubble		Several	Fail
Market experts		Fear long term	Neutral
Politics		Trump	Fail
Misc.		Trade war	Fail
		Overall	**Fail**

[1] This is the market timing technique without using a chart.

[2] I tried to use SMA-400% to reduce false signals without success.

[3] Get it from http://www.multpl.com/ Same as CAPE.

[4] Get it from https://www.ici.org/research/stats. It is based on 09-12-18. "Flow to Equity" is based on domestic ETF estimate. Treat it as two phases in moving to equity. First phase of moving excessively to equity indicates the market is peaking. The second phase indicates the market is plunging when flow of equity is excessively negative.

[5] Global corporations will suffer in profits converted back to USD and hard to sell to foreign countries. [4] Get it from the above link.

[6] Rising interest is bad for corporations and high-ticket products, but good for lenders.

[7] Get it from

https://www.treasury.gov/resource-center/data-chart-center/interest-rates/Pages/TextView.aspx?data=yield based on 09/21/18

[8] With the low interest rate, it may not be that critical. Corporations take advantage of the low interest rate.

Overall

Overall, technical is fine as the market is making new highs. Many aggressive investors exit the market on technical indicators only as the over-valued market could linger on for a long term such as from 2009 to 2017 so far.

Overall, fundamental is not sound. The increasing market price also is decreasing the fundamental metrics such as P/E, P/B and P/S. It is bad unless there is reason to support such as the fast earnings growth in 2009.

Many metrics are deteriorating

RSI(14) is getting closer to 65 (a passing grade specified by me).

Inverse yield curve (1.5 vs. 2.33) is about 61% apart from my interpretation and calculation. It is not a warning now but we should keep an eye on it. Most market crashes have occurred when it is 0% or negative. The theory is that in a normal case the short-term interest rates should be lower than the long-term interest rate.

Another source calculates it is 1.1% and that is very close to inversion since the last recession. From MarketWatch, the 30-year fixed interest rates is 4.66% and 1-year rate is 3.96% giving an inverse yield curve 18% apart, which is quite alarming.

Mathematically incorrect, today's full employment is at 4%. Most recessions are closely preceded by troughs in unemployment and the reverse for economy recovery.

GDP growth has been predicted from 1.8% to 3%. The 3% is from the White House for their obvious purpose. I predict it will pop up due to meeting the tariff deadlines, tax cuts and spending increases. It will then be declining to 2%. A healthy US economy should maintain 3% without special factors such as excessive immigration.

We have record debts: investors' margin, corporate debt and Federal debt. These are bubbles going to burst. Federal debt / GDP is about [95%](https://fred.stlouisfed.org/series/gfdegdq188S) today. It does not predict the market performance as this ratio was 53% and 55% before the last two market crashes. It will affect the long-term performance of the economy when we have to service the huge national debt.

We do have 10 years of stock growth at the expense of record Federal deficit. Thanks to President Obama from investors and no thanks from next generations who have to pay back our national debt. It is overdue for a correction. Hopefully it is not a crash which has an average loss of about 45%. We did have two recent corrections losing more than 10%: 2011-12 EU debt crisis and 2014-16 oil crash. The oil price has been rising from $30 per barrel to today's $70. It is still a long way from my warning of $120.

Potential triggers
Trade wars with China, Canada or EU will be the strongest trigger. Our most profitable companies are virtually all international companies. They need fair trade to prosper.

The other trigger is the possible impeachment of President Trump.

Check the validity of our charts
It seems some metrics vary. It could use after hour trading. It could be the "Days" may be "Sessions" – calendar day is different from trading session. I selected 10 years for most of the charts and StockCharts let me select only 5 years.

Here is a list of sites for charts.
https://www.stocktrader.com/2013/12/10/best-free-stock-chart-websites/
These are the three sites I use a lot: Fidelity (customers only), StockCharts and Finviz.com (missing some metrics).

As stated before, SPY may not be the best to represent the market. I prefer an ETF for 1,000 stocks and weigh the stocks evenly (i.e. not according to the market cap). Google "market timing 2020 (or current year)" for more expert info. Here is one.

Mid-year update

Basically nothing significant has changed recently: The market is fundamentally unsound and technically sound after the recent rally. The only update is our national debt is skyrocketing. Today's "Debt/GDP" is similar to the market height in 2000 and we know what happened afterwards. That's why Buffett has accumulated a lot of cash now.

Even with the unlimited QE (i.e. printing money excessively), the high inflation and market crash predicted by many experts have not been materialized so far. This is my third prediction in "Disaster of 2020". The status of USD as a reserve currency will be shaken; I do not know when, as I do not have a time machine.

Why the market keeps going up while the economy is going down? The Fed has provided a lot of cash and the cash is chasing a fixed number of assets such as gold and stocks. It is the simple, proven theory of demand and supply. It will continue for a while as long as there is unlimited supply of money. At some point, it will pop. At that time, it could lead to a long recession, unless the economy improves as it did in 2009. The smart Fed chairman knows how it will harm the country by excessively printing money. However, he has to obey his boss who is seeking for reelection.

I expect we are in a prolonged period of low interest rates and even negative interest rates. When the rates are negative, our Treasury bonds are no longer marketable. The foreign central banks including China would dump our national debts if it has not been already started. The economy is dressed up nicely in an election year. Giving us free money is the easy way to buy votes, but the long-term effects are very harmful.

Using cheap money to buy back the company's stock would boost the stock price and hence make the management wealthier. It is a false sense of the stock value. When the company cannot pay back the debt obligations, the company would go bankrupted. If the U.S. were a company, she has gone bankrupted already.

As of 6/15/2020, QQQ (representing NASDAQ stocks) has been up 11% YTD and it is far better than DIA (representing DOW stocks) and SPY (representing the 500 large stocks in the S&P Index and losing about 5% YTD). QQQ has a lot of tech stocks while DIA has a lot of losers including Boeing. Most FAANG stocks are making record highs and QQQ is market cap weighed.

Most of the ETFs on chips have been up more than 40% in a year. I bought Amazon and two chip ETFs. I use trailing stops to protect my portfolio. Huawei is buying a lot of U.S. chips in the 120-day relaxed period. In September this year and if there is no extension, I would sell these chip ETFs fast.

I have used the strategy described in my book "Profit from the recovery of the pandemic" to take advantage of this volatile market. I used 5% as the threshold and I had too few trades; now I changed to 3%. Expecting a market crash, I weigh more on contra ETFs. As described in the same book, I bought a lot of contra ETFs, GLD and the stock of a gold miner. It is for insurance. ETFs on oil is my big mistake.

If the U.S.D. loses the status of reserve currency (not likely soon), it would bring prolonged depression and high inflation in the U.S. In this case, it is safer to invest in real estate, precious metals and profitable companies than in CDs and bonds that would lose values due to inflation.

Check out many articles on the status of the current market. Many have opposing views, so you have to make your own decision. In any case, play it safe with stops. Here is one article from MarketWatch.com.

Canary warning?

When I was working on my new book "Best stocks to buy for 2021" on Dec. 10, 2020, I found something really strange. I have never rejected so many stocks that have Fidelity's Equity Summary Score higher than 9. I rejected them as there were a lot of dumping from the insiders. Insiders know their companies better than most of us. Is it the canary telling us the market is over-valued?

Initially the following stocks have been screened by my value screens. Buy any one of the following stocks, **only** if you have good reason(s).

Symbol	Fidelity Score	Insider Purchase
BCC	9.9	-24%
GPI	10.0	-17%
HEAR	10.0	-75%
HIBB	9.4	-30%
HVT	9.5	-37%
HZO	9.5	-27%

How can HEAR score a perfect 10 while the Insiders' Transaction is -75% (I treated -2% is normal). The analysts must be wrong this time, or they believe the market will continuously make new heights. Will update the performance results later to see who is wrong.

A correction or a crash?

In Dec., 2018, the S&P500 is about 15% down and a crash is about 45% down.

If a crash is coming, there should be additional 30% down. If it is a correction (15% average), then we have it already. Should we pick up bargains now? Or, are they bargains? It is a trillion dollar question.

We need a trigger for a market crash like the financial crisis in 2008 and the internet bubble in 2000. Besides the record-high margin debt, the possibility of Trump's impeachment and a trade war, I do not see any.

Filler: CIA mistook it as a missile silo in China.

2　Market timing by calendar

The following predictions are based on historical data. You may have slightly different findings depending on when you start and when you end your testing.

You can load the historical data of SPY via Yahoo!Finance and check out how close you are or different from my own predictions. They are my predictions based on historical data. Use it as a reference only.

- Presidential cycle.
  Usually the market performs worse in the first two years after the election than the next two. During the 3rd year the president has to make the economy look rosy in order to buy votes. Statistically it is the best year for the market and is followed by a good year (the election year). The government may stimulate the economy, the stock market and employment by printing more money, lowering interest rates and lowering taxes. The market in the 100 days before the election should be positive and less volatile according to 40 years of data.

  Democratic presidents have better market performance statistically than Republican presidents. This is not too logical as though Republicans are more pro-business traditionally.

- Olympics.
  It has been proven that the host country has a better chance that its stock market appreciates the year after the Olympics. It could be due to the exposure from the Olympics and / or the huge expenses in preparing for the Olympics.

  The last two Olympics follow this pattern as of 12/23/2013:

Olympics Country / Year	ETF	Period	Return
United Kingdom / 2012	EWU	Jan. 3, 2013 - Dec. 23,2013	11%
China / 2008	FXI	Jan. 3, 2009 - Dec. 31, 2009	43%

  Greece could be an exception. It is too small a country to host this world-class event and it has wasted too many resources by building too many white elephants that the country can never justify. Brazil depends on its export of natural resources to China, so I do not count on the Olympics effect there.

Winning a lot of Olympic medals has no prediction for the stock markets. Both the Russian Empire and E. Germany were winners but disappeared in their original forms afterwards.

- Seasonal.
  Best profitable investment period is: Nov. 1 to April 30 of the following year. It is similar to the saying 'Sell in May and Go away'. It did not work since 2009 as it was an Early Recovery (defined by me) in the market cycle.

  The market does not always happen as predicted. However, when more folks follow this, it becomes a self-fulfilling prophecy. I prefer "Sell on April 15 and come back on Oct. 15" to act before the herd. The more practical strategy is to start selling in April 1 and become more aggressive (selling at closer to the market prices) when it is close to May 1. For the last five years, I did not find this prediction reliable.

  The explanation of the 'summer doldrums' could be that the investors cash their stocks for vacations and college tuition in the fall. Buying quality companies at the dips could be profitable.

- The worst month: September.
  The next worst month is October. However, if there is no serious market crash during October (and this month has more than its shares of crashes), it could be the best month to buy stocks.

- The best month for the bull: November.
  However, several market bottoms occurred in October and November. The next strong month is December.

- Best 30 days: Dec. 15 to Jan. 15, next year.
  It was correct for the period of 2012-2013.

- Window dressing.
  Institutional investors sell their losers and buy winners around Nov. 1. From my rough estimate and on the average, the winners have a 2% percentage point gain better than the market and the losers have 1% worse than the market.

I recommend that you evaluate the top 10 winners from the last 10 months or YTD in Oct. 15 and sell them at 3% gain or two months later.

I recommend that you buy in Dec. and sell them 3 months later. Include the stocks with more than 30% loss for the last 11 months or YTD, sort them by Earning Yield in descending order and evaluate the top 10 stocks.

In both cases, do not buy foreign stocks and stocks with return of capital. Ignore stocks not in the three major exchanges, with low volumes and stock prices less than $2. Do not buy in losing years such as 2007 and 2008. I have my tests with my own assumptions and I use tools not available to most readers.

This is a guideline only. Do not buy any stocks during market plunges. Current events should be considered first such as a potential war and the hiking of interest rates.

Afterthoughts

- I predict it will be a sideways market in the later part of 2013. I am following the sideways strategy: Buy on dips and sell when the market is ups. One's prediction.

- Why September has a bad reputation?
  http://www.marketwatch.com/story/betting-on-septembers-terrible-odds-2013-08-27?dist=beforebell

The September of 2013 (2 days away at the time of this writing) will have more problems. Check it out how many of the following are correct on Oc. 1, 2013. Use it as a future guideline to predict the next September using the current market conditions then:

1. The market is not excessively expensive, but it is not cheap. It is due for a 5% correction.
2. Unrest in Syria (check any unrest in your next prediction on September).
3. High oil prices due to Syria.

4. September is statistically a bad month for the stock market. However, it could be an opportunity to invest after the correction if any.
5. Interest rates is rising.
6. All the above indicate the market will dip. However, the rosier outlook is that the global economies are improving even slowly.

- January effect.
  The performance of January may determine how the entire year performs. I cannot find any rationale but it has been proven right statistically.

- Earnings period announced in Jan., April, July and Oct. would cause big swings in stocks when they have surprises. Earning revisions could be a good predictor.
  http://www.investopedia.com/terms/e/earningsseason.asp

Links
Presidential Cycle:
http://www.investopedia.com/articles/financial-theory/08/presidential-election-cycle.asp

Calendar-based market timing:
http://stock-chartist.com/2010/10/calendar-based-market-timing/

Calendar market timing for 2013:
http://www.investorecho.com/archives/8047

Filler: Golden Gate

Just minutes ago, my mail system asked me to sign in. I did and repeatedly they asked me to sign in again and again. I closed down everything and followed Gates' golden rule: If everything does not work, just power down everything and power it up again. I did this and prayed too. It works. Thanks Gates for fixing my problem.

There is NO one doing BASIC quality control. If it happened in my generation, many guys would be fired. Mediocrity is the new norm?

3   Politics and investing

You may ask why politics is discussed in this investing book. Politics has been proven to affect the market. For example, the market had reacted to the different stages of Quantitative Easing whose dates had been preset. The following is a more recent example.

I predicted 2015 would be a year with small profit and insisted on so even during the fierce correction in August. Why I was so sure? Very seldom the market is down in a year before an election year including 2007. The last occurrence was 1939, the year when WW2 started. Investing is a multi-discipline venture including statistics and politics. It may not always happen, but the probability is high for these years.

How to profit

2015 was a sideward market. The market reacted to good news and bad news. The strategy for sideway market is: Buy at temporary downs and sell at temporary peaks. Define 'temporary' according to your risk tolerance.

For the 'temporary market down', personally I used 5% down from the last market peak. To me the 'temporary market peak' is 10% up from the last market down. The percentages can apply to the percentage changes in the stocks in your watch list. In another words, I buy the stock when the market is 5% down from the last peak and sell it when it gains 10% or the market gains 10%. Be reminded that this strategy is opposite to market plunges, where you should exit the market totally - again depending on your risk tolerance.

The following are my purchases on 08/26/2015. I should have bought more stocks and one day earlier if I were not blinded by fears (a human nature) during this correction. Here is my proof for my purchase orders. The four stocks were described as value stocks in a SA article and I did a simple evaluation. As of 12/31/2015, I sold all the four stocks except Gilead Sciences. The annualized returns are more impressive such as GNW's 10% gain in one day.

Stocks	Buy Price	Buy Date	Return	Sold date

Apple (AAPL)	107.20	08/26/15	12%	10/19/15
Gilead Sciences (GILD)	105.94	08/26/15	-4%	
General Motors (GM)	27.69	08/26/15	12%	09/17/15
Genwealth Financial (GNW)	4.54	08/26/15	10%	08/27/15

There were similar examples in 2013 and 2014.

2016: Politics and the market

No one including all the Federal Reserve chairmen / chairwomen and all the Nobel-Prize winners in economics can predict market plunges. One chairman predicted a smooth market and a few months later the housing market crashed. Many predicted correctly market crashes by pure luck. One even received a Nobel Prize and became famous. However, you are glad to ignore his later market predictions.

There are at least two best sellers asking us to exit the market in 2009. If you followed them, you would miss all the big gains from 2009 to 2014. They did have a point. However, you cannot fight the Fed. The market had been saved by the excessive printing of money and hence created a non-correlation between the market and the economy. I bet these authors (famous economists and gurus) may have not made a buck in the stock market. It is a classic case of the blind leading the blind.

From their articles, they do not know the basic technical indicator. You only want react to the market when the market is plunging and not too early. That's why most fund managers cannot beat the market as most are not allowed to time the market. Buffett had mediocre returns in the last three years – I had warned my readers three years ago in my blogs/books. To me, the 'buy-and-hold' strategy is dead since 2000. The average loss from the peak for the last two market plunges is about 45%. Most charts depend on falling prices, so you will not save 45% and 25% loss is my objective.

Fundamentally speaking

The market in 2016 is risky due to the proposed interest rates hike, our record-high margin, strong U.S. dollar and the high expenses of the wars to start. Each reason could be a good-size article. Personally I try to maintain 50% in cash and would flee the market if my technical indicator tells me so.

Politically (and statistically) speaking

The election year is the second best for the market, but it may not be this year. We seldom have three terms from the same political party. For that, I predict a win by the Republicans. Republicans are usually pro-business, but ironically the democratic presidency has better track record for better market performance.

The market has more than recovered since the day when Obama took office. The S&P500 performance under Republicans vs. Democrats since 1926 to 2014 is approximately:

Annualized return under Democratic presidencies: 13%
Annualized return under Republican presidencies: 6%

The market is riskier based on the above statistics. In addition, there is a good chance that we will have either a non-politician president or a lady president for the first time. The market usually does not favor to this kind of change.

Critical political issue for 2016

On our way back at about 4 pm on a Saturday, the bus was full of Spanish-speaking workers. I bet most are illegal workers working in my suburb such as our malls, the hospital and many restaurants. Why illegals? I bet most legal folks would get welfare instead of working in that shift. If they work, the state would take away the freebies such as health care in Mass. The illegals do not have this option. I do not think the politicians understand this. There is no need for building a border wall but punishing the employers who hire illegals. Before we do this, we need folks to take the jobs taken by the illegals today.

What will happen if the politicians turn the illegals to be legal? There will be nobody doing these jobs I predict. No one in the right mind wants these jobs as it is far easier to collect welfare. Why would politicians make this stupid decision? They want to buy Hispanic votes as evidenced in the last two elections.

In addition, most politicians side with the welfare recipients. Since 40% of the population do not pay Federal taxes, the politicians have to satisfy their needs in order to buy votes.

We should encourage folks to work, not the other way round. Representation without taxation is worse than taxation without representation.

Our high taxes, regulations and strong US dollar dampen our competitive edge.

Some political decisions/regulations that affect the stocks

Beside the presidency and the interest rates hike(s), there are many political decisions and regulations that affect the stocks. Just name a few here:

- The never-ending wars postpone our secular bull market beyond 2018.
- Solar City (SCTY). It depends on government energy credit.
- My Chinese solar panel stock evaporated when the US banned them from importing to the US.
- Any gun control measurement will affect gun stocks.
- Restrictions on cigarettes.
- France imposes extra taxes to foreign investors.
- Government bailouts on 'too big to fall' companies.
- Corporate taxes boost the exodus of corporation headquarters to tax heavens for the US. It is the same for Chinese corporations.
- Infrastructure projects.
- Taking out the ban to export oil would increase the profits for oil companies.
- After the annexation of Crimea, the Congress restricted using Russia's rocket engines and gave new opportunity to the US companies in this

area. Besides political consideration, Chinese rockets are the most cost effective and more reliable.
- China's suppressing corruption affected Macau's casinos...

Summary

Politics affect the market. I predict a risky market in 2016.
Economy and religion also affect the market. Statistically speaking, the market is ahead of the economy by about 6 months. However, the current market is an exception. The correlation will return to normal.

Religions cause wars as the ones in the Middle East today. These huge expenses are consumption, not investing. It will not be good for most sectors of the economy especially in the long run.

Written in 1/1/2016.

Note.

Predictions are predictions. However, the more the educated the guess is, the better chance the guess will materialize. My technical indicator gave only one false alarm from 2000 to 2009. It happens more often after that period. The market is far more volatile than before. In most cases, false alarms will not hurt at all except tax consequences on taxable accounts. The false alarm tells us to exit the market and come back shortly.

Appendix 1 – All my books

- Complete the Art of Investing (highly recommended combining most of my books on investing). The Kindle version has over 850 pages (6*9).

- Sector Rotation: 21 Strategies (highly recommended for short-term investors) has more specific chapters on the topic and shares many articles with "Complete the art of investing".

- Best stocks for 2021. Not a promise: Another "Best stocks" books available on July, 2021 and Dec. 15, 2021.

- China: "Apocalypse or Co-prosperity (highly recommended). Trade War (most popular here) with China. Trade War & Pandemic. Rising China. Fall of an Empire: U.S.A. A Nation of No Losers. Can China Say No. Global Economies. Pandemic.

- Books for today's market: Profit from Coming Market Crash.

- The following books are in a series: Finding Profitable Stocks, Market Timing and Scoring Stocks. Alternate book Using Fidelity.com.

- Books on strategies: Shorting, "Profit from bull, bear and sideways markets" (Rotation + Momentum + ETF Rotation + trend following), Trading System (similar to printed version of Complete), Swing (Rotation + Momentum), ETF Rotation for Couch Potatoes, Momentum, SuperStocks, Dividend, Penny & Micro Stock, and Retiree.

- Books for advance beginners: Introduce (highly recommended), Billionaire (perfect gift for recent college graduates and they will thank you when they become millionaires), Investing for Beginners, Beat Fund Managers, Profit via ETFs, Buffett, Ideas, Conservative and Top-Down.

- Miscellaneous: Lessons in Investing. Investing Strategies. Buy Low and Sell High. Buy High and sell Higher. Buffettology. Technical Analysis. Trading Stocks.

- Concise Editions and Introduction Editions are available at very low prices and are competitive with books of similar sizes (50 pages) and prices ($3 range).

Most books have paperbacks. Links and offers are subject to change without notice.

Appendix 2 – Complete the Art of Investing

Instead of buying 16 books, why not buy one book (Complete the Art of Investing) consisting of 16 books? Besides saving money and your digital shelve space, it gives you quick reference and concentration on the topic you're currently interested in. It covers most investing topics in investing excluding speculative investing such as currency trading and day trading.
The Kindle version has about 850 pages (6*9), about the size of three books of average size. With the cost of $10 and at least 850 investing ideas, it is about one cent per idea. Most other books have only a few ideas in the entire book

The 16 books

This book "Complete Art of Investing" is divided into 16 books as follows. Click for the link to the book described in Amazon.com. I squeezed more than 3,000 pages into 850 pages by eliminating duplicated information such as evaluating stocks.

Book No.	Amazon.com
1	Beginner & Billionaire
2	Finding Stocks
3	Evaluating Stocks
4	Scoring Stocks
5	Trading Stocks
6	Market Timing
7	Strategies
8	Sector Rotation
9	Insider Trading
10	Penny Stocks & Micro Cap
11	Momentum Investing
12	Dividend Investing
13	Technical Analysis
14	Investing Ideas
15	The Economy
16	Buffettology

The book links are subject to change without notice.

"How to be a billionaire" is for beginners and couch potatoes, who can use the advanced features of this book in the simplest and less time-consuming techniques. Most advance users can skip this section unless they want to use some of the short cuts described.

We start with the basic books Finding Stocks, Evaluate Stocks, Trading Stocks and Market Timing. You can select and start with one of the many styles and strategies in investing such as swing trading and top-down strategy. Many tools are described in other books such as ETFs, technical analysis, covered calls and trading plan.

Many books start with "Why" to lure you to read more and are followed by "How" and then the theory behind the book.
If the book you're reading is beneficial to you, imagine how it would with 850 pages.

\#

Most readers' comments are on "Debunk the Myths in Investing", which this book is originally based on.

"I skipped ahead to his chapter book 14 (of "Complete the Art of Investing"), Investment Advice just to get a feel of his writing style. His research is phenomenal and doesn't overwhelm with big words or catchy "sales-like" tactics.

I truly believe this ordinary man, Mr. Tony Pow, has a gift of explaining his experience as an investor without the bull crap of trying to make you buy his stuff. He seemingly just wants to share his knowledge, tips, and clarity of definitions for the kind of folks like me who want to understand something FIRST before jumping in with emotions of trying to make a boat load of money. I like the technical analysis side he brings.

Mr. Tony Pow talks about hidden gems in his book; well....quite frankly, he is a hidden gem. Thank you and I will also post my comments about this author to my Facebook page!" – JB on this book.

"Excellent book, recommend to all investors… great knowledge. It has fine-tuned my investing strategies… Your book is hard to set aside, as I read it all the time learning good techniques and analysis of stocks, ETF…

Since I purchased your book in March, I have underlined, highlighted and placed tabs on top of pages for quick reference." – Aileron on this book.

"Tony, I just finished reading your 2nd edition. It's my pleasure to report that I found it most interesting. You're welcome to use this blurb if you like:

Debunk the Myths in Investing is an all-encompassing look at not only the most salient factors influencing markets and investors, but also a from-the-trenches look at many of the misconceptions and mistakes too many investors make. Reading this book may save not only time and aggravation but money as well!"

Joseph Shaefer, CEO, Stanford Wealth Management LLC.

"Tony, Great work!" from James and Chris, who are portfolio managers.

"'Debunk the Myths in Investing' is a comprehensive book on investing that deals with many aspects of this tense profession in which with a lot of knowledge and a bit of luck (or vice versa) one can greatly benefit...

Therefore 'Debunk the Myths in Investing' is an interesting book that on its 500 pages offer a lot of knowledge related to investing world and many practical advice, so I can recommend its reading if you're interested in this topic."
- Denis Vukosav, Top 500 Reviewers at Amazon.com.

"490 pages (Debunk) of a genius's ranting and hypothesis with various theories throughout, written light-heartedly with ample doses of humor...Yes, the myth of not being able to profitably time the market is BUSTED...

One might ask... Why is he giving away the results of his hard-earned research for only $20? He states that his children are not interested in investing and wants to share his efforts with the world." - Abe Agoda.

"Excellent book, recommend to all investors... great knowledge. It has fine-tuned my investing strategies... Your book is hard to set aside, as I read it all the time learning good techniques and analysis of stocks, ETF... Since I purchased your book in March, I have underlined, highlighted and placed tabs on top of pages for quick reference." - Aileron on this book.

"Great stuff, Tony. It's great to meet experienced traders such as yourself. I had a browse through the book and think your method is a little more refined than mine."
"Your strategy is very rules based and solid. I sometimes envy people who have developed something like this."

Making 50% in one month
I claim to have the best one-month performance ever for recommending 8 or more stocks without using options and leverage. My following return is 57% in a month or 621% annualized. They are slightly different as I calculated the average from the averages of three different accounts. The average buy date is 12/26/18 and the "current date" is 01/28/19.

The performance may not be repeated. I will use the same screen for the coming years and even the expected 10% (or 120% annualized) is very good.

I used the same screen for searching stock candidates. I spent a total of about 20 hours from Dec. 15, 2018 to Jan. 5, 2019.

Stock	Buy Price	Sold or Current Price	Buy date	Sold or Current date	Profit %	Profit % Ann.	Status
CHK	2.13	2.99	01/03/09	01/18/19	40%	982%	Sold
MNK	16.41	21.45	01/03/19	01/25/19	31%	510%	Sold
MNK	16.43	21.45	01/03/19	01/25/19	31%	507%	Sold
NNBR	5.68	8.58	12/26/18	01/28/19	51%	565%	
NNBR	5.72	8.58	12/26/18	01/28/19	66%	727%	
ESTE	4.35	6.45	12/26/18	01/18/19	48%	766%	Sold
LCI	4.61	8.29	12/21/18	01/28/19	80%	767%	
MDR	8.01	9.13	01/08/19	01/28/19	14%	255%	
YRCW	3.29	5.78	12/21/18	01/28/19	76%	727%	
YRCW	3.26	5.78	12/21/18	01/28/19	77%	742%	
ASRT	3.56	4.18	12/26/18	01/28/19	17%	193%	
UTCC	7.13	11.00	12/26/18	01/28/19	54%	600%	
YRCW	2.92	5.78	12/26/18	01/28/19	98%	1083%	

Best one-year return
I claim to have the best-performed article in Seeking Alpha history, an investing site, for recommending 15 or more stocks in one year after the publish date without using options and leverage.

Your choice

"Complete the art of investing" should be your first choice. "Sector Rotation: 21 Strategies" and "Sell Short Stocks /ETFs" are your better choice depending on how often you rotate sectors or selling short. All three books share most articles. "Best Stocks" select the stocks for the period. "Be a stock expert in 5 minutes" and "Beat the fund managers" are books for beginner investors. "China and U.S." is my book on politics.

Sector Rotation: 21 Strategies

- On 5/26/2020, I searched for "Sector Rotation" under Amazon's Book. They are listed in the same order except my book Sector Rotation: 21 Strategies.

Book	Date	Size[1]	Kindle $[1]	Hard $
Sector Rotation: 21 Strategies	**05/2020**	**425**	**$9.95**	**$24.95**
Super Sectors	09/2010	289	$26.39	$49.95
Dual Momentum Investing	11/2014	240	$40.40	$42.20
Sector Investing	05/1996	260		$29.94
Sector Trading Strategies	08/2007	164	$26.39	$16.66
The Sector Strategist	03/2012	225	$26.39	$44.96
ETF Rotation	10/2012	125	**$9.95**	**$14.99**
Optimal... Sector Rotation	07/2015	80		$44.07

[1] From Amazon on size and prices as of 5/25/2020.

My book won in all categories except the price for hard copy in one. However, my book won as the lowest cost per page by a wide margin. In addition, as of 5/2020 I bet that no author besides me made over 4 times using sector rotation starting the amount more than his yearly salary then.

- I have **21** strategies in sector rotation while most books have only one. It ranges from simple rotation of a stock ETF and cash for beginners to many advanced strategies for experts. Most other books have one or two strategies.

- Andrew, a contributor on Sector Rotation article at Seeking Alpha, said, "Great stuff, Tony. It's great to meet experienced traders such as yourself. I had a browse through the book and think your method is a little more refined than mine."

- "You have written the book in a way that makes good and logical sense." Bill.
- Do not be fooled by past performances. Just check the recent performance of the top 50 stocks selected by IBD in the last five years. The mediocre result (hopefully it will change) could be due to too many followers and/or there is no evergreen strategy. I seldom heard the fantastic results from the followers of O'Neil, our greatest chartist. The adaptive strategy of this book shows you how to select the most profitable strategy for the current market.
- I switched most (if not all) my sector funds in April, 2000 from technology sectors to traditional sectors (better to money market fund). We can reduce losses by spotting market plunges and the sector trend.

My motivation to write this book is sharing my experiences, both bad and good. I provide simple-to-follow techniques using the free (or low-cost) resources available to us. I have been successful in investing for decades. I am enjoying a comfortable financial life. I do not hold back my 'secrets' as my children are not interested in investing. If you are looking how to make 100% return overnight, there are many other books claiming to do so and this book is not for you. This book describes how to be a 'turtle' investor making fortune gradually and surely. Be warned that many books written by authors who have never make money in the stock market.

Best stocks to buy for 2021

We care about performance only. The last book beats the market (SPY simulating S&P500 index) by 29%. Click here for the book or type the following for more info on the book.
https://www.amazon.com/dp/B08Q8R6SXQ

This is the performance of my last book "Best Stocks to buy from August, 2020". Past performances do NOT guarantee future performances.

The performance is the returns from 07/28/2020 to 12/07/2020. The average of the 14 recommended stocks beats SPY (an ETF simulating S&P500 stocks) by 29%. There are 13 winners and 1 loser. Dividends have not been included. CMCSA and FDX are big winners profiting from the pandemic.

Symbol	Name	Sector	True EY[1]	Return[2]	Ann. Return[2]
ABBV	AbbVie	Drug	7%	10%	27%
ABT	Abbott	Drug	3%	8%	21%
CHE	Chemed	Diversified	4%	4%	12%
CMCSA	Comcast	Media	11%	19%	52%
FDX	FedEx	Transport	8%	76%	211%
GTS	Triple-S	Health	N/A	26%	72%
JNJ	Jonson & J	Drug	6%	2%	4%
MCK	McKesson	Drug	8%	16%	45%
MSFT	Microsoft	Software	4%	6%	18%
SCHN	Schnitzer	Metal	10%	46%	127%
SMCI	Super Micro	Computer	11%	9%	24%
UFPI	Universal	Building	10%	-6%	-17%
UNH	United Health	Health	9%	15%	43%
ZBRA	Zebra Tech	Computer	5%	39%	107%
Avg.				19%	53%
			SPY	15%	41%
	Beat SPY by				29%

[1] True EY is the reciprocal of "EV/EBITDA". [2] Rounded up for easy reading, but not in the calculation in "Beat SPY by".

It is not a promise: I may have a similar book after 7/1 and 12/1 every year. Check my blog. https://tonyp4idea.blogspot.com/

Sell Short Stocks / ETFs

Book	Date	Size	Kindle $	Hard $
This book (Sell Short Stocks /ETFs)	**10/2020[1]**	**700[2]**	**$9.95**	**$26.95**
Short selling with the O'Neil Disciples	04/2015	336	$31.99	$43.22
The New sell & sell short	03/2011	368	$20.79	$31.57
Sell Short	03/2009	240	$18.39	$26.88
Sell and sell short	05/2008	250	N/A	$43.21

China and U.S: Apocalypse or Co-Prosperity

On 11/2020, I searched for "Trade War China" under Amazon's Book. They are listed in the same order except my book. This represents and summarizes most of my books on politics.

Book	Date	Size[1]	Kindle $[1]	Paper $
This book	**12/2020**	428	$4.95	$14.95
The U.S. – China Trade War: Conflict	**10/2020**	302	$9.95	$14.99
Us Vs China: From trade war…	09/2019	346	$11.59	$28.00
The China-US. Trade war and future economic relations	12/2018	222	$39.00	$39.00
Stealth War	10/2019	255	$7.95	$18.29

You have been brainwashed by our government and the media on China that has been demonized every day. I can say the same to the Chinese in China. My book is a summary of all my books on politics and hopefully represents the unbiased views from many overseas Chinese. That is why we have conflicts between the two countries.

Appendix 3 - Our window to the investing world

The paperback version of this chapter can be found in the following link.
http://ebmyth.blogspot.com/2013/11/web-sites.html

- **General**
  Wikipedia / Investopedia /Yahoo!Finance / MarketWatch / Cnnfn / Morningstar /CNBC / Bloomberg / WSJ / Barron's / Motley Fool / TheStreet
- **Evaluate stocks**
  Finviz / SeekingAlpha / MSN Money / Zacks / Daily Finance / ADR / Fidelity / BlueChipGrowth / Earnings Impact / OpenInsider / NYSE / NASDAQ / SEC / SEC for 10K and 10Q (quarterly) reports required to file for listed stocks in major exchanges.
- **Charts**
  BigCharts / FreeStockCharts / StockCharts /
- **Screens**
  Yahoo!Finance / Finviz / CNBC / Morningstar /
- **Besides stocks**
  123Jump / Hoover's Online / FINRA Bond Market Data / REIT / Commodity Futures / Option Industry
- **Vendors**
  AAII / Zacks / IBD / GuruFocus / Vector Vest / Fidelity / Interactive Brokers / Merrill Lynch /
- **Economy.**
  Econday / EcoconStats / Federal Reserve / Economist /
- **Misc.**
  Dow Jones Indices / Russell / Wilshire / IRS / Wikinvest / ETF Database / ETF Trends / Nolo (estate planning) / AARP /

Appendix 4 - ETFs / Mutual Funds

What is an ETF

ETFs have basic differences from mutual funds: 1. Lower management expenses, 2. Trade ETFs same as stocks, and 3. Usually more diversified but not selective than the related mutual funds such as NOBL vs FRDPX.

The major classifications of ETFs are 1. Simulating an index such as SPY, QQQ and DIA, 2. Simulating a sector such as XLE and SOXX, 3. Simulating an asset class such as GLD and SLV, 4. Simulating a country or a group of countries such as EWC and FXI, 5. Managed by a manager(s) such as ARKK, 6. Betting a market or sector to go down such as SH and PSQ, and 7. Leveraged (not recommended for beginners).

Fidelity: Index ETFs (https://www.fidelity.com/etfs/overview).

Wikipedia on ETF (http://en.wikipedia.org/wiki/Exchange-traded_fund).

List of ETFs

ETF Bloomberg
http://www.bloomberg.com/markets/etfs/
ETF data base
http://etfdb.com/
ETF Trends
http://www.etftrends.com/
A list of ETFs. Seeking Alpha.
(http://etf.stock-encyclopedia.com/category/)

Fidelity's commission-free ETFs. Check current offerings and whether they are still commission-free.
(https://www.fidelity.com/etfs/ishares)

Fidelity Annuity funds with performance data.
http://fundresearch.fidelity.com/annuities/category-performance-annual-total-returns-quarterly/FPRAI?refann=005

A list of contra ETFs (or bear ETFs)
http://www.tradermike.net/inverse-short-etfs-bearish-etf-funds/

Misc.: ETFGuide, ETFReplay (highly recommended).

Other resources
Your broker should have a lot of information on ETFs and many offer commission-free ETFs.

Most subscription services offer research on ETFs. IBD has a strategy dedicated to ETFs and so does AAII to name a couple. Seeking Alpha has extensive resources for ETF including an ETF screener and investing ideas.

Not all ETFs are created equal
Check their performances and their expenses.

Small but well-performing ETFs

Here is a list.
http://finance.yahoo.com/news/small-etfs-pack-big-punch-195430875.html

Guggenheim Spin-Off ETF (CSD) looks interesting. The ETF tracks corporate spinoffs. It has beaten SPY for a long time; check the current performance. Not a recommendation.

When not to use ETFs

I prefer sector mutual funds in some industries but you need to do extensive research. They are drug industry, banks, miners and insurers.

Half ETF

Taking out half of the stocks that score below the average in an index ETF could beat the same full ETF itself. I call it HETF (half the ETF). You heard it here first.

To illustrate, sort the expected P/E (not including stocks with negative earnings) in ascending order and only include the stocks on the first half. Add more fundamental metrics. It will take a few minutes.

Disadvantages of ETFs
- When you have two stocks in a sector ETF one good one and one bad one, the ETF treats them the same. Stock pickers would buy the one that has a better appreciation potential.
- The return is better than the actual return due to stock rotation. To illustrate this, on August 29, 2012, SHLD was replaced by LYB in a sector fund. SHLD was down by 4% and LYB was up by 4% primarily due to the switch. Unless you sell and buy at the right time (which is impossible), your return would not match the ETF's returns due to the replacement.
- Ensure the performance matches the corresponding index, but will most likely not include dividends.

Advantages of ETFs
- We have demonstrated that you can beat the market by using market timing. Between 2000 and Nov., 2013, you only exit and reenter the market 3 times and the result is astonishing.
- It is easy to rotate a sector vs. buying/selling all of the stocks in this sector. It makes sector rotation the same as trading a stock.
- The risk is spread out and your portfolio is diversified especially for a market ETF or buying three or more ETFs in different sectors.
- Eliminate the time in researching stocks.

Leveraged ETFs
I do not recommend them. Some are 2x, 3x and even higher. They're too risky. However, when you are very sure or your tested strategy has very low drawdown, you may want to use them to improve performance. I recommend skipping all leveraged ETFs.

My basic ETF tables

I use a list of selected ETFs and commission-free (check the details) ETFs from Fidelity for my purpose. I include some mutual funds in Fidelity's annuity. Some of these may be interesting to you. I use ETFs for sector rotation and parking my cash when the market is favorable and I do not have stocks that I want to buy.

ETFs and funds come and go. Some ideas and classifications are my own interpretation.

Table by market cap:

Category	ETF	Fidelity ETF	Mutual Funds	Fidelity's Annuity	Contra ETF
Size:					
Large Cap	DIA		See Blend		DOG
	SPY				SH
	QQQ	ONEQ			PSQ
	RYH				
Blend	IWD	IVV	BEQGX		
Growth	SPYG	IVW	FBGRX		
Value	SPYV		DOGGX		
Dividend	NOBL	DVY	FRDPX		
	VYM				
Mid Cap				FNBSC	MYY
Blend	MDY	JJH	VSEQX		
Growth		IJK	STDIX		
			BPTRX		
Value		IJJ	FSMVX		
Small Cap				FPRGC	SBB
Blend	IWM	IJR	HDPSX		
Growth		IJT	PRDSX		
Value		IJS	SKSEX		
Micro	IWC				
Multi					
Blend			VDEOX		
Growth			VHCOX		
Value			TCLCX		
Bond					
Long Term (20)	VLV		BTTTX		TBF
Mid Term (7 – 10)	VCIT		FSTGX		
Short Term (1 – 3 yrs.)	VCSH		THOPX		
Total	BOND		PONDX		
Corp Invest Grade	VCIT		NTHEX		
High Yield (junk)	PHB		SPHIX		
Muni	MUB		Check state		

Special situation					
Buy back	PKW				

Table by sectors:

Sector	ETF	Fidelity ETF	Mutual Funds	Fidelity's Annuity
Banking[1]			FSRBK	
Regional	IAT			
Bio Tech	IBB		FBIOX	
	XBI		Large	
Consumer Dis.	XLY	FDIS	FSCPX	FVHAC
Consumer Staple	XLP	FSTA	FDFAX	FCSAC
Finance	KIE	FNCL	FIDSX	FONNC
	IYF			
Energy	XLE	FENY	FSENX	FJLLC
Energy Service			FSESX	
Gold	GLD		FSAGX	
Gold Miner	GDX		VGPMX	
Health Care	IYH	FHLC	FSPHX	FPDRC
	VHT		VGHCX	
House Builder	ITB		FSHOX	
	ITB		Perform	
Industrial	IYJ	FIDU	FCYIX	FBALC
Material	VAW	FMAT	FSDPX	
	IYM			
Oil	USO			
Oil Service	OIH		FSESX	
Oil Exploration	XOP			
Real Estate	VNQ		FRIFX	FFWLC
REIT	VNQ			
Retail	RTH		FSRPX	
	XRT			
Regional bank	KRE		FSRBX	
Semi Conduct	SMH			
Software	XSW		FSCSX	
	IGV			
Technology	XLK	FTEC	FSPTX	FYENC
	FDN		FBSOX	

			ROGSX	
Telecomm.	VOX	FCOM	FSTCX	FVTAC
Transport	XTN			
	IYT			
Utilities	XLU	FUTY	FSUTX	FKMSC
Wireless			FWRLX	

Footnote. [1] Also check Finance.

Table by countries outside the USA:

Country	ETF	Fidelity ETF	Mutual Funds	Fidelity's Annuity
Australia	EWA			
Brazil	EWZ			
Canada	EWC		FICDX	
China	FXI		FHKCX	
EAFE	EFA			
Emerging	VWO		FEMEX	FEMAC
Europe	VGK		FIEUX	
Global	KXI		PGVFX	
Greece	GREK			
India	INDY		MINDX	
Indonesia	EIDO			
Latin America	ILF		FLATX	
Nordic			FNORX	
Hong Kong	EWH			
Japan	EWJ		FJPNX	
S. Africa	EZA			
S. Korea	EWY		MAKOX	
Singapore	EWS			
Taiwan	EWT			
	TUR			
United Kingdom	EWU			
Foreign:				
Combination	1	2	3	4
Intern. Div.	IDV	DWX		
Small Cap	SCZ	GWX		
Value	EFV			
Europe	VGK			

#Filler: Honey, my book can play music.
https://www.youtube.com/watch?v=HxGT5z6d-GA&list=PLMZa6mP7jZ2b1otqG4tfbgZpLEdh6YiNF

It may cut down commercials by casting it to TV.

www.ingramcontent.com/pod-product-compliance
Lightning Source LLC
Chambersburg PA
CBHW051539170526
45165CB00002B/801